FINDING BEAUTY
in the
GRAY

STORIES AND VERSE
FROM THE THIRD AGE

HUGH J. WILLARD

ISBN: 978-1-960146-79-3 (hard cover)
      978-1-960146-80-9 (soft cover)

Edited by: Melissa Long and Hannah Cohen

Warren publishing

Published by Warren Publishing
Charlotte, NC
www.warrenpublishing.net
Printed in the United States

To Wally Willard, my dad, a deeply wounded man
who impressed upon me the values of perseverance and resourcefulness

AUTHOR'S NOTE

To survive, you must tell stories.

—Umberto Eco

Y
ou have in your hands—be it on paper or your digital device de
jour—a book of stories. *Which vessel do these stories come in*, you
may ask? Well, in this time, wherein "genre-blurring or bending" is
the haute couture of the literary and music industries (among others),
this book can be considered a collection of nonfiction essays with a
couple of fictional vignettes thrown in for good measure. A smattering
of poems serves as the pitch to buoy this craft on the prevailing seas
of life in the Third Age. Namely, the trade wind themes of identity,
reevaluating meaning, purpose, relationships, and an exploration of
creativity in the second half of life.

*Wait a sec, if this is a work of nonfiction that addresses these themes, wouldn't
we call this a self-help book?*

If you must consider it to be so, then so be it. Just please don't speak
it aloud in my presence. We'll agree to disagree. I have spent my
professional lifetime as a psychotherapist digesting reams and tomes
of self-help, and I must admit, there have been some truly good ones,
life-altering even. But for every one of high value, there are hundreds
of formulaic retreads and pablum that follow a similar format:
introduce an issue or concept, offer a brief anecdote to bring color to
said concept, sprinkle in a few statistics, and liberally throw around the

phrase "evidence-based practices" for the bulleted list of prescriptions to cure what ails you. While you will find some similarities in this book, the departure happens largely in the arena of prescription, directive, and pathology. The Third Age is not inherently a problem to be fixed. Yes, there are challenges, expected and not, but this time of life is floral and fecund, or at a minimum, it can be. We seasoned adults have an abundance of capacity and experience upon which to draw to attend to the trials as well as to amplify the joys. I allow—or, more accurately, get out of the way and let—the stories and poems serve as enzymes to your own integrative process. Perhaps this is what Umberto Eco and many others have in mind.

What's the big deal about being given the straight poop? Being told what to do? Well, do you remember the old maxim about giving a fish versus teaching to fish? For quite some time, we've been handing out fish to people with the result being that our attention spans have been alarmingly shortened. And, to throw in another clichéd phrase, we walk around with one tool, a hammer, and we end up seeing a lot of nails.

For the whole of my life, I have been a story person. In truth, we all are, but for me, story has been a palpable, forceful driver of my experience. In relatively equal parts teller and listener, story has been the container for my relationships, personal and professional. In my early years, I tilted more toward "storyteller" only to see this skew shift to "listener" after college. Over the past thirty-plus years, I have had the honor of sitting with individuals as a counselor, holding their stories with great respect, and helping them to heal, whether through resolution or integration and acceptance. To counsel suggests giving advice. To counsel well, one must first listen. In moments of my clients' journeys, after listening, it has been fitting for me to share anecdotes, some of which have been pieces of my own story.

Moving further into the latter half of my life, I'm sensing a pull, an urge to bring forth some of these stories, to share with the greater community. This is often considered the exclusive trade for memoirists, both famous and unknown, and lest we cheapen this calling into clichéd and voyeuristic entertainment, I'd like to point to the value and importance of sharing our stories with others.

In my early years, I often heard the phrase, "I have to get home to watch my stories." This was the refrain of the adults who religiously spent their afternoons watching the daytime soaps. These shows were frequently lampooned for the over-the-top depictions of the lives of the characters or, should I say, "caricatures." These storylines took the very common trials and tribulations of everyday life and condensed and bastardized them into sideshow carnival fare.

Authentic stories—our stories, yours and mine—are the connective tissue that binds and reinforces our relationships. These stories, time-tested, have had their debuts on the backs of napkins in dimly lit bar corner booths, in preschool sandboxes, on the stoops of big city apartments on hot summer evenings, in the bleachers of high school football stadia on chilly October nights, and even in the backs of hay-less trailers bumping along in apple orchards in the mountains of North Carolina—as you will read about in the first section of this book. They help us to see and know each other. They cultivate compassion. Our stories are gifts of learning, legacies that serve us, our family, and our friends.

Like astrophysics to the universe, neuroscience is making fast, firm advances in understanding the seemingly fathomless wells that are our brains. One area that has held particular interest is memory. Our memories, we are coming to understand, are composites of experiences, shaped and added to with each turn of recollection. This has important implications in many areas of our lives. Dramatically, we think of memory's role in courtroom settings, with eyewitness accounts often being the thread upon which a prosecutor's case hangs.

On a more practical and immediate level, memory is vital to our understanding of ourselves, our relationships, and our environments. We draw upon our memory to remind us of lessons learned, lest they be painfully and unnecessarily repeated, joys we seek to engage again, loves lost, and reminders of our value and place in the broader scheme.

Memory serves as the evidence for us to answer meaningful questions of our integrity to our interests, commitments, and to the people and things we value deeply. I'm reminded of the heart-rending scene at the close of the movie *Saving Private Ryan*. The elder Ryan is standing before the white cross of Captain Miller, who died in the mission to rescue him. Private Ryan stares pleadingly at the marker and says, "Every day, I think about what you said to me that day on the bridge. I tried to live my life the best that I could. I hope that was enough. I hope that, at least in your eyes, I've earned what all of you have done for me."[1] Once again, a very dramatic rendering of the role of memory. While most of us don't lead lives deemed Hollywood-worthy, they are, nonetheless, our lives and, as such, are not to be considered less valuable. To ourselves, our loved ones, and our communities, our experiences matter and are essential squares in the patchwork quilt of humanity.

It seems a cruel twist that, as we age, all the while garnering more experiences and adding to the composites of ourselves, some of our memories blur. It is in the crosshairs of this dynamic that we need to lean into the essence of story, trusting we retain the learnings that continue to serve us and our loved ones near and far, though various details may ebb and shift. Indeed, one of the graces of story is it may be manifested in many forms—traditional and non—in essay, poem, sketches, wordless melody, architecture, and artifact just to name a few.

An example of the essence of story is my earliest "memory." I was less than a year old and already a pro at climbing out of my crib. Once liberated from my crib, not yet walking, I would scamper off in a fast crawl in pursuit of exploring parts unknown. The world was vast and endless, and I had much to discover. Prior to the event in question, I would be discovered and repeatedly returned to my holding cell. On this one fateful day, I climbed out of my crib and made my way to the basement steps with the door ajar. Moments later, following a series of thumps, thuds, and graceless somersaults, I lay on the cold cement floor, near my father and grandfather, who were working on a long-forgotten project. This is all I remember of that event. Not because I was knocked unconscious. Rather, because that was where the story, as told many times by my parents, always ended. They would add a cursory, "Everyone was horrified, but you were okay." I heard the story enough times to form an actual memory of the event, a visual of my experience that sits nicely in the hippocampal region of my brain.

It is highly improbable my stored memory is anywhere close to the reality of the experience. The essence of this story, however, fits quite consistently with numerous other events throughout my childhood and beyond, ones I actually *do* remember. I am an explorer and, as illustrated in my earliest story, always have been. I learn, as most of us do, by various means, but for me specifically, the chief among these is by doing. I would place this learning style in the "high risk, high reward" category. I far and away led my family in trips to the ER and certainly also suffered my share of emotional cuts, breaks, and bruises. But it was and is this wanderlust that served as the life force fueling my conscious pursuit of knowing myself and the world around me, which continues to this day.

And for each of us, however we pursue continuing insights into ourselves and the world, we are now needing to integrate the experience and impact of a global pandemic and heightened domestic and geo-sociopolitical strife. In the face of these unprecedented (in modern times) events, we crave the familiar. It's human nature to do so. We work so hard to manage changes, losses, and the threats of a future impoverished of touch, economic security, and seeing or being seen. Story is the essential tool for us to carry forward onto these untrodden grounds, both the external, the post-pandemic land before us, and the interior, our individual journeys into the latter years of our lives.

In the following pages, I will share stories in various forms that touch on the aforementioned themes. I have sat with countless individuals and couples, bearing witness to their descent from the heights of career and family life to the level, if not unfamiliar, surface air of retirement and post-childrearing years. The strength of this book rests on their backs. They come from many walks of life, crossing cultural and socioeconomic bounds and life circumstances. I am grateful to them for their willingness to be vulnerable with me, for opening the door into their joys, but also their pains, losses, and fears. We are all the better for their courage in sharing their stories.

Regarding their stories, I will often change names and identifying details to honor their rights to their own experiences. It is the essence of their, and my, stories that I hope will contribute to the respective journey of you, the reader.

PART I
Who Are You, Really?

Here's a test to find out whether your mission in life is complete.
If you are still alive, it isn't.

—Lauren Bacall

Geoff is an old friend who is living his best, authentic vintner life. He has had more than his fair share of adventures and wounds over the course of his fifty-nine years. Geoff came to his craft and passion for winemaking following a winding, nondescript career in the sales world, one he would call "middling." In his late forties, following some unexpected personal upheaval, he hit the eject button on his sedimental (pun intended) life and went to school to learn about vinification. I asked him about wines and the aging process. He noted that most wines are made to be enjoyed relatively soon; most wines are not supposed to be laid down in a cellar to mature for years, much less decades. Contrary to the accounts we hear about in the movies spoken with that certain air of sophistication—"This is a 1787 Chateau Lafite, sir!"—the wines will get old and spoil. He further said that for the wines to age well, bottles should be laid down on their side but then spun in regular increments to keep the cork moist. He finished with, "Beyond these factors, aging wine takes time. Not years and years, but still, to do it correctly, you must be very patient."

When I initially conceived the idea for this book, beyond my clients, I drafted a survey that I sent out to Third-Agers before interviewing them. I wanted to hear more about their experiences of identity, meaning, relationships, and creativity at this time in their lives. The survey began with the requisite name, rank, and serial number. The very first question I asked after this demographic set was, "Who are you?" I didn't intend for this to be a trick question, but the first several people to complete the survey repeated what they had just given me three lines above: their name.

I'll grant that a personal name is most powerful. On some meta scale, it forms the transcendent label that encompasses all the internal associations and experiences that comprise the whole of each of us. Our surnames are an extension of this to include our collective family and heritage. This has a power all unto itself and takes us in the direction of legacy.

But those associations and experiences have defined limits when viewed via the lens of the other. Say I meet you at the proverbial cocktail party, and, lacking the proper social graces, I blurt out, "I'm Hugh Willard." And then, before you can collect yourself, I fix my piercing stare and ask, "Who are you, *really?*" After you gather yourself, you would probably tell me your name—or avoid eye contact and mutter something about needing to find the restroom as you slip away. However, if I more politely introduce myself, I will likely follow this up with the genial standard, "What do you do?"

There have been many musings about the limiting character of this question, namely that we usually consider this to be primarily about our vocational role. This is understandable in our free-market, first-world lives. So much orients to our utility. It's the lead on our *Wikipedia* pages, were we to have ones, even in retirement, even posthumously.

How might it be if the next time you are asked who you are, you respond with your name, followed by any litany of other defining pieces of yourself? "I am Hugh Willard. I am a son of deceased parents, a father, a partner, a brother, a creative, a retirement coach and therapist, a writer, and a musician." I could conceivably talk for five minutes or more and only partially answer that question. *Being* (who I am) and *doing* (the manifestation of who I am) are interesting constructs for us to consider our identity. Furthering this consideration is the container that is time. The older we get, the more used-to-be phrasings show up in our thoughts and conversations.

I used to be an engineer.

I used to be a good singer.

I used to be an avid gardener.

To state the obvious, the words *used to be* signal the cessation of both being and doing. In other words, they describe artifacts. And while artifacts do have a role for informing the present experience and our sense of self, let us endeavor to remember we are still living and growing so we can, indeed must, counterbalance the *used-to-be* side of the scale with the *I-am-now* side and even the *I-intend-to-one-day-be* side.

Like good wines, irrespective of the intended lengths of our lives, as we age, we need continued tending and turning to bring us to the fullness of our character. In this first section, we will take in stories and experiences that reflect on the themes of identity and meaning in the Third Age.

When you retire, if you had a busy job, you take your busy-ness with you.
                                                    —BILL CARSON

The Blue Ridge Parkway offers a welcome summer respite from the stifling, muggy flatlands of central North Carolina. Each year, with temperatures a good seven to ten degrees cooler and lower humidity, it beckons a steady throng of visitors to its myriad attractions. The unadulterated, quiescent grandeur of the land itself would be more than enough to entice me. Growing up in the North Carolina Piedmont, I've spent parts of every summer and winter traipsing and trolling around this whispered wonderland. Feeling well-versed in the Blue Ridge's offerings, I was delighted to come across something new one bright July morning in 1999. Where there was once a long-neglected scrabble of parched, brittle, and lichen-covered apple trees, there was now a vibrant, fecund expanse of an orchard, aptly named the Orchard at Altapass.

Not long after pulling in to check out this revived botanical bevy, I found myself with a handful of other guests in the back of a dusty wood-paneled trailer being pulled by a large John Deere tractor, a good old-fashioned hayride minus the hay.

As we toured the orchard, sitting at the fore of the trailer and facing us was an avuncular, bespectacled gentleman with a worn denim baseball cap and an easy, accent-less speech pattern. Bill Carson, one of the founders of the Orchard at Altapass, began spinning stories of truth and lore about the orchard and surrounding lands. One particularly amusing anecdote was about the McKinley patriarch from the 1800s, whose name was assigned to a nearby gap that ran along the majestic ridges. As Bill told it, Mr. McKinley was quite peripatetic and purported to have had many wives and more than one hundred children across the hills, which provided convenient distance and natural cover for his antics.

Bill Carson is a natural storyteller. A peaceable man, his soft eyes and unassuming façade belie his rail-straight and steady locomotion. He is a man with purpose and vision. As a child, he watched the Sputnik space launch on TV with his dad, and his fate was sealed. His newfound love of math and science took him to Purdue University and a degree in engineering, which he parlayed into a thirty-two-year career with IBM. He had central roles with NASA and all the moon shots.

With Apollo 11's historic mission and Neil Armstrong's iconic small step, humankind began a consummated love affair with outer space that continues to this day. Over the years, we have learned the merest or most prolific amount, depending on one's perspective, about the outer realms. Bill's hands were on the engineering side. On another side, we learned quickly about the mental and physical effects of going from a gravity-laden environment to a gravity-less setting and back again. There is the potential for muscle, bone, and organ atrophy, among other possible deleterious impacts. Given these insights, NASA and other space agencies have learned how to properly prepare and acclimate astronauts to the venture from one planetary-scape to another. This includes a precise protocol immediately following splashdown for the astronauts. Depending on the duration of the mission, it can take anywhere from a few months to a year to readjust to life back on Earth.

Bill eventually finished his work with NASA before moving over to a few other projects, including working on the Patriot Missile program for the Department of Defense. He was indeed a busy man.

And then Bill retired in 1993 at age fifty-four.

Fortunately for Bill, he had foresight and intention that accounted for and allowed him to take his busy-ness with him into retirement to ease the splashdown and steps into a life beyond. The impact of moving unprepared too quickly into this new time and setting were not to be. A lifelong, healthy financial steward along with his wife Judy, Bill knew they were on solid financial ground as he moved into his fifties. What was left for Bill was finding purpose and outlets for creative pursuits.

He and Judy loved Colorado. They bought a cabin in Durango and imagined settling into a life of baking cookies for the tourist passengers at the railroad depot in Silverton. Two years before retirement, when this plan failed to gain sufficient traction, Bill pivoted and bought a loom.

He began teaching himself the craft of weaving, in time creating beautiful and intricate art. He shared the story of deciding to take one of his creations to a craft fair in the North Carolina mountains. He and Judy had moved there by this time. They loved the area and were tending to his ailing aunt. He was musing over what price point would be reasonable for his wall hanging. "I considered that I probably spent about sixty hours on the project. I decided that ten dollars an hour sounded okay, so I said six hundred dollars." At the fair, several folks stopped and admired his piece, but no one seemed interested in buying.

Bill then described one lady who complimented him on the rug. "She looked at the price tag and misread it, saying, 'Sixty dollars? That's too much!'" Bill smiled and told me, "It was at that moment I realized I was weaving for myself."

In 1994, Bill's sister came to the mountains and, through sheer serendipity or divine providence, fell into buying a certain declining apple orchard on the Blue Ridge Parkway. While this purchase was occurring, Bill was looking for additional meaningful pursuits and, given his interest in the stars and planets, was considering building an astronomy unit to place atop his house. But, in his words, "this would have been a terrible idea."

Once his sister had purchased the orchard, Bill's latest path and purpose lay before him. He and Judy became intricately involved in operations oversight, helping to revive the orchard and develop it into a central cultural hub for preserving the waning traditions and values of the mountain people: patience and forbearance, perseverance in the face of difficulty, sitting and being present to and with others, hard work, and the sacredness of the land. With thousands of people annually visiting the Orchard at Altapass—who come not only to buy apples but also to hear traditional mountain music, dance, and take one of Bill's famous hayrides through the orchard while he shares stories handed down through the centuries—Bill has found his purpose. He talks of the from-heres and the not-from-heres being able to mix at the Orchard. He talks of using his busy-ness to help others. And he talks of dancing.

Bill also wanted to be a dancer. He even took lessons … *four* times. "After the fourth round," he says with a wry smile, "the instructor quit." Bill, however, soldiered on.

A friend eventually gave him the simplest of instructions. "Bill, make sure a foot hits the floor on every beat. It doesn't matter which one, as long as one hits the floor on every beat."

Bill notes he is still dance-challenged but frames it this way: "I'm not good but not intimidated."

In keeping with his good humor, the Orchard has printed bumper stickers that read, "I survived a dance with Bill Carson." During my visit, Bill, again with that quick, subtle smile, even pulled out a business card saying the same thing. He then shared a more touching story of a young woman who was a frequent visitor with her parents to the Orchard. Bill asked her to dance, and with encouragement from her parents, she finally consented. Afterward, Bill saw tears in the eyes of the young woman's parents. They shared that their daughter had autism and would never have done something like that before. As a postscript to this story, Bill said the woman is now a dance instructor at an annual autism camp in the mountains. "Saving the good stuff" is Bill's oft-invoked saying, referring to the preservation of the mountain values.

All along the way, through his graduated descent from the high altitude of a most successful and engaged IBM career, Bill has calibrated to this latest plane of life. Allowing my metaphor mixing, Bill has mastered the craft of weaving community through the Orchard. The warp (from-heres) and the weft (not-from-heres) coalesce into a beautiful, original art to be rightfully displayed. Bill found himself the latest significant, essential part of the composite he had been creating across his whole life.

★★★

The Third Age
I want to learn how to ice skate.
I find myself with an hour of free time,
Perhaps two.
I could rest, no one should fault me if I did
Although there is a tottering mound of dishes cresting the lip
of the sink.
I have spent a lifetime of cooking, and cleaning, and eating.
A lifetime of crumbs baked into the plates.

I found a pair of skates, worn and wan,
Burrowed in a bin at the thrift store.
I spied the first soft tan heel
Under a chipped, marble-black bowling ball.
The flat shine on the blade of the other skate
Jutting out from a soiled Raggedy Ann's embrace.

I could take my hammer to the Habitat house.
No child should be without a home,
Although the constant electric stabs
At the base of my gnarled fingers
Remind me of many a driven nail
And point to younger hands more suited for this.

The skates I found are just my size.
Sure, they could use some TLC,
Maybe a caress and some coconut oil,
But they'll do just fine.

I'm not trying to match the poise and élan
Of a pirouetting gold medalist.
My beauty has its own pace and name.

I could read the digital news feed,
But what would I learn about the world
That I don't already see and feel daily?
There is much pain, and much love too,
Warbling and intermingling
Like a morning chorus of songbirds
Folding around the wrench of the crow's caw.

I could meet my friends down at the park.
An autumn woods walk, breathing the wisps of smoke
From the nearby homestead would be nice,
Feeling myself meld into yellow maple leaves
Slows my heart and thickens my eyelids.
But would I hear what my friends are saying?

I feel the cool air dampen my eyes.
The ribbed ice at the outdoor rink
Speaks of the coming winter.
The glide and grace, the blade and balance
Find the natural curves and sways
As my skin tingles anew.

In the end, she became more than what she expected.
She became the journey, and like all journeys, she did not end;
she simply changed directions and kept going.

−R. M. DRAKE

The state flower of Texas, the bluebonnet, is a purple- and blue-hued species native to the Southwest United States. The petals resemble the bonnets pioneer women wore. After Lady Bird Johnson and her husband left the White House, as one of many beautification projects she had overseen, the former first lady was instrumental in encouraging the planting of these native flowers along the highways in Texas. In an interview in 1993, Charles Kuralt asked, "When you come right down to it, it's a good deal of trouble to plant wildflowers. What good do they do?" "Just joy," was her response, "and joy is a component of life, or should be."[2] Today, it is a common sight to see a line of cars just off a North Texas route in early spring. Admirers take family pictures in magical, florid fields of the previously quiescent creatures in their full April glory. I was told of this generations-old tradition by Sandra, a lady who very much reminded me of Lady Bird Johnson.

I had the pleasure of chatting with Sandra at a dinner party several years ago. Like the former first lady, Sandra was self-made, charitable, curious, clear-eyed, and ambitious. A woman of singular intellect, light and affable, yet deliberative in her discourse. A fellow Texan. A doer. Sandra considered it her obligation to give back and pay it forward, a similar sentiment to Lady Bird Johnson, as described by her granddaughter, Lucinda Robb: "That [planting wildflowers] was going to be her way to pay her rent for the space she took up on the planet."[3]

Sandra once shared with me a Native American story about the origin of the bluebonnet. She said the tribe's chief had asked for the sacrifice of an important possession to the Great Spirits. A young girl, She-Who-Is-Alone, was the only one who came forward, offering her beloved doll, a gift from her deceased parents. The Great Spirits were pleased, admiring the girl's bravery and sacrifice. The rains came, followed immediately by an overflowing field of bluebonnets. The bluebonnet has thus come to symbolize this bravery and sacrifice.

Sandra was a college president for many years. Like Lady Bird, since leaving her post, Sandra has repositioned to numerous other endeavors, including full-time research and writing. She delighted in sharing with me a photo album of pictures from her latest trip back home to Texas. She was visiting her brother, who owns a wildflower farm, and working on a new project about native flowers. She was good enough to share the absolutely resplendent pictures of bluebonnet fields. She added that nowhere else on Earth can one find these treasured beauties.

Hearing Sandra describe her latest venture following the end of her tenure at the college, I shared my book project, describing my work with issues germane to the retirement years and how I had stumbled across a label known as *recareer* that had a new footing in the Third-Age lexicon. The term refers to the recent uptick in persons engaging in new work after a long tenure in a previous career. I told her I didn't really care for that word, as it suggests going back into something confining or laborious for some people. She quoted Rita Mae Brown in response: "Language exerts hidden power, like the moon on the tides."[4] And then she went on to say she preferred the term *reposition*, which connotes a turning to something different.

Words matter. Archaeologists go on digs to unearth the pottery shards and the exoskeletal remains of building columns and everyday tools of former civilizations. This goes a long way toward helping us learn the ways and means of these ancient societies. But if you want to glimpse the sinew and flesh of a culture, look *inside* the exoskeleton, and there you will find words. Words are more than mere two-dimensional symbols to mark different items and actions in our environment. Language is alive and evolving, often in very subtle ways, belying our beliefs and prejudices, our hopes and fears. Words can expand and uplift or constrict and sink. Language saturates our psychology, our thoughts, creating positive momentum (growth) or negative momentum (atrophy). What words occupy the most bandwidth for you? Your family and friends? While acknowledging and allowing for the importance in validating hard and distressing experiences, consider how each use of a limiting word or phrase adds another pebble, or boulder, to the decaying side of the scale, just as a generative word or phrase adds a pebble, or boulder, to the healing side of the scale.

Is it *past my prime* and *out to pasture*, or is it *a new day* and *one foot in front of the other? Back in my day* or *seize the day? Can't* or *I'll try?*

Lady Bird Johnson's daughter Lynda Bird said of her mother, "She was very, very disciplined with her language but very loving. Words were kisses from her."[5]

For many, the word and experience that is *retire* suggests a change in focus away from production and growth, into a life of ease and pleasure. But is there a Siren-like trap in this conditioned thought and picture? Does this mentality unwittingly contribute to decline after the retirement honeymoon? In modern English, *retire* literally means "to tire again" … okay, maybe I made that up, but you know that is what we hear. *Retire* derives from the Middle French word *retirer*, which means "to withdraw."[6] I understand its application in that we "withdraw" from a lifetime of work, but this can feel like negative momentum.

Mihaly Csikszentmihalyi wrote *Flow: The Psychology of Optimal Experience*, a seminal book in the world of modern psychology. He talked about our best moments as being when we are challenged and stretched. He made an interesting distinction between pleasure and enjoyment. Pleasure, Csikszentmihalyi said, helps to maintain order. There is an understandable place for this in our lives. But, according to Csikszentmihalyi, enjoyment goes beyond pleasure, to include achieving something possibly unexpected. It's about growth and change. It will often include pleasure but will most often include challenge first.[7]

Bluebonnets are hardy annuals. They have a penchant for reseeding themselves, ensuring a glorious return the next year. Lady Bird Johnson reseeded herself after five challenging and rigorous years in the White House. Sandra reseeded herself after many years in the field of higher education.[8] There is an important time and place for fallow fields, but this should always be in the service of replenishment so our fields may bear beauty once again.

★★★

A flag, at a minimum, represents an idea, an identity. More fully, like the coat of arms, a flag tells a story via color, image, and motto. The latest incarnation of the US Marine Corps flag, dating back to 1939, has a scarlet background with a golden-colored eagle atop a globe set inside an anchor. A white, undulating banner below reads, "United States Marine Corps," and clamped within the beak of the eagle, a smaller, white banner waves over the top of everything. This one says, "Semper Fidelis," which is Latin for "always faithful" and the credo for every Marine. It signifies the dedication each Marine has to the "Corps and country." It is a way of life. It is an uncompromising code of integrity to ethical and moral behavior. It is steadfast loyalty.

It was a breezy, late March morning when I met a new neighbor named Ron. I was out for my morning walk when I came upon him at the edge of his yard. He was tossing manure mulch about the ring of sharp, yellow daffodils and the riotous rainbow of tulips by his mailbox. I grinned and commented on how I loved the smell of cow shit in the morning. This play on the hackneyed line from the movie *Apocalypse Now*—"I love the smell of napalm in the morning"—was not lost on him.[9] He gave a slight perfunctory smile and cast his eyes down. His straw-like gray hair frayed out from under his dark-blue baseball cap with a gold-trimmed Marine insignia. I then noticed the red-and-gold Semper Fi sticker on the back of his mid-2000s Ford

Escort wagon. Given his likely age, my attempt at icebreaking humor was possibly poorly timed and placed.

Jutting out from the side of a porch post was a mildew-speckled, wooden flagpole, one where an American flag is commonly flown. However, in its place was a white-trimmed flag waving and tussling in the March wind, with a picture occupying much of the frame. I could just make out that it was a silkscreen print of children. After introducing myself, I asked Ron about the flag. His eyes gleamed as he told me they were his grandchildren. He shared how he spent ten years in the Marine Corps, retiring as a master sergeant. While he was proud to have served his country and is appreciative of the expressions of gratitude he gets from others, he added that being a veteran was no longer enough for him.

"It doesn't help me get out of bed in the morning," he said. "Point of fact, as much as I hate to say it, it's been a real struggle for me. Don't get me wrong. I love my country and would do anything to defend her. Semper Fi is forever in my bones. But doing time in 'Nam did a number on me. It ain't easy for me to talk about. Cost me my marriage and my kids for a time. Made it hard to keep jobs." Then he pointed to the photo flag on the pole. "Being Pop Pop to these crumb-snatchers, that's what keeps me going. I get to take them to school every morning and pick them up every afternoon, to help their mother. They're my happiness. Semper Fi is for more than just the Corps and country."

Over the course of many early-morning walks, I learned more about Ron. Mostly, we talked about landscaping, vegetable gardening, and cars. And, of course, the grandkids. There was an ease in Ron's voice when he talked about his grandchildren. He would speak of masterful first-grade art projects, or maybe the feat of the youngest balancing on one leg for an inestimable seven to eight seconds before tumbling into Ron's lap. Over time, knowing I am a therapist, he occasionally circled the edges of his combat experience with me, unevenly tightening into the sphere of trauma. I sensed there was a limit to how far these particular conversations would go.

I learned his father was a Marine who had served in World War II. Ron revered his father, but I could hear the cumulative effect the war had on his dad, the impact that passes to the next generation. The alcoholism, the drifting from job to job, and the lack of meaning and focus in his father's life.

Holocaust survivor and Austrian psychiatrist Viktor Frankl witnessed the unspeakable horrors of the Nazi concentration camps throughout the war. Out of this experience, he engaged his life's work, and we are all the better for it. In his book *Man's Search for Meaning*, he talked of the necessity for each person to identify personal purpose in their day-to-day lives. While this, he observed, helped him and some of his fellow Jews to survive the horrendous conditions of captivity, he noted it is just as important for the likes of you and me today. [10]Our meaning doesn't have to be on the scale of Semper Fidelis, nor does it have to be noble by anyone else's standards; it just has to be authentically ours. Along with identity, it becomes our Polaris, our North Star.

Less poetically, identity and purpose are the chicken and the egg. One begets the other.

Speaking of identity, suffice it to say, we weave and wear many outfits over the span of our lifetimes. Some senses of ourselves are core—son or daughter, sibling, parent, or some religious or philosophical identity. Some are significant for a time—student, military service member, engineer, homemaker, friend, technician, and teacher. And some are more transient—HOA board member, holiday parade volunteer. Logically, it follows that the more central an identity is in our lives, the greater the impact when it changes or ends. We often greatly anticipate crossing the finish line of our career. Spending decades in one or several vocational pursuits is nothing to sneeze at when we consider the effect, and affect, of punching the clock for the last time. We can get excited about sleeping in, taking up tai chi, and going for that gondola ride in Venice. But how well do we consider all the additional time that collects like so many coins under the couch cushions?

I'm not dismissing that many Third-Agers are keenly tuned in and grateful for the opportunities to live renewed and meaningful lives. But how that translates and is applied in real time to our lives in retirement is of utmost importance. A recent MetLife Retirement Readiness Index Study found that 62 percent of those interviewed retired without any idea of how they would craft a life in, or adjust to, retirement.[11] For many of us, this Third-Age time is a marathon, not a sprint. We need to ensure we are intentional in our self-inventory and exploration.

We may consider Tom Cornish to be an ultra-marathoner. Tom is a ninety-six-year-old Minnesotan with a lifelong history of volunteer service. He began by volunteering to join the Navy at age eighteen, serving in the South Pacific during World War II. He then returned to Minnesota and volunteered for various groups and causes while working and raising five children with his wife Lorraine. Following her death, Tom remarried and continued his passion for serving others. Tom and his service came to international attention amid the early days of the COVID-19 pandemic.

During the time of greater sequestration, he began weaving hats. His initial goal was to do one each day. He often exceeded this number, and by the time his efforts were discovered by the media, he had completed over four hundred hats that were, in turn, donated to the Salvation Army. In addition, he taught others in his senior-living complex the craft of weaving hats, and the number multiplied.

"If someone needs something, give it to them," Tom replied when asked about his efforts. "Volunteering does something to a person. You're working for others."

His son Jerry added, "This is how he got to be ninety-six years old. Because he's helping everyone else."[12]

Since we are inherently social beings, there is no authentic purpose that can be or remain insular. Anything we aspire to do or to be must have at least some focus and destination beyond ourselves. A commitment to someone, something, a group, or an idea that directly or indirectly serves someone or something outside ourselves. The source of this aspiration may come from our family or community or religious faith. It may come unbidden, seemingly from a place of interiority. Irrespective of the source, our happiness and well-being are directly proportional to the degree we clarify and engage our life's purposes. Given the guarantee of slights and wounds and challenges in our lives, pursuing authentic purpose is an unerring compass for the path ahead.

★★★

I was out on a walk recently when I came upon Ron. It happened to be the morning of July 7. I had not seen him for a few days. The prominent dark circles under his eyes greeted me. He shook his head and said, "Did you hear all that ruckus last night? I mean, I get it on the Fourth. I understand that people love their fireworks. Forty-five years later and I still get spooked by those damn things. At least I *know* it's coming on the Fourth, and I can prepare myself. But c'mon, people. There's no sense in this mess going on three to four days later."

Just then, a towheaded boy opened the front screen door. "Pop Pop? Can we have pancakes for breakfast?"

Ron turned toward his grandson, stretched his arm, and offered a soft wave. "Sure, son. I'll be there in a minute." Ron's shoulders opened and dropped as he smiled. "The kids are over for the week."

Sometimes, we find our peace through direct resolution; always, we find our balance through meaning.

★★★

Ecclesiastes V3 Redux

To everything, there is a season
Seasons are ultimately simultaneous
One earth rotating around the sun
In summer and spring, in fall and winter.

Our job is to teach, and to learn
To listen, and to talk
To be authentic, and to make mistakes
To love, and to be afraid
To rest and to toil
To play and to persevere
To fight for peace.

Seasons are omnipresent and fleeting
Jacob's circular staircase ascending and descending.

Our place is to unify, and to break down
To find meaning, and to distract ourselves
To accept and to deny
To live in aesthetics and asceticism
To share and to covet
To touch the sacred and the profane.

What is the purpose of living paradoxically?
The willow's roots are firm, strong, and aggressive
The tree is pliant, with wispy tips, and shimmery,
   light leaves
The bark an unending source of elixir.

Born whole into a broken world
Each calling is universal
To set about the journey of integration
Which is itself a contagion of healing and wholeness to
   begin anew.

In Shel Silverstein's book *The Giving Tree*, a poignant and beautiful story unfolds about the relationship between a boy and a tree. The story follows the boy's comings and goings, and the tree's repeated self-sacrificial acts in pursuit of serving the boy's happiness. This tracks throughout the boy's life, reaching the climactic end when the boy, now an old man, takes his rest on the stump of the once towering, vibrant tree:

> "I wish I could give you something … but I have nothing left. I am just an old stump. I am sorry …."
> "I don't need very much now," said the boy, "just a quiet place to sit and rest. I am very tired."

"Well," said the tree, straightening herself up as much as she could, "well, an old stump is good for sitting and resting. Come, Boy, sit down. Sit down and rest."

And the boy did.

And the tree was happy.[13]

The story and associated illustrations are quick, simple, and heart-tugging. I remember reading this book to both my girls when they were young. It was several years later when I finally caught up to the unhealthy undertow that carries through the story. The boy used the tree for his own self-centered interests, only to leave each time until the next need arose. This was my clinically astute "ah-ha" moment.

And yet, despite it all, there was love. The story begins with imperfect love, and the story ends with imperfect love.

I've long loved willow trees for their soft beauty, their associations with healing, and their penchant for bearing up under harsh circumstances. Another tree that captures my fancy is the river birch, native to the Eastern United States. Its flecked, curled, and mottled bark of tan, sienna, and burnt umber has a beauty all its own. A little-known character of the river birch is that its roots grow in rough, imperfect heart shapes. Among the varied hardwoods, some trees are more amenable to root anew from cuttings and proper care. The river birch is one of these.

I recently reconnected with an old friend. Barbara and I worked together as school counselors back in the early '90s. When we first met, I was quickly impressed by her wit, determination, and dedication to her students. She is as deep and plainspoken as a Mary Oliver poem. She has no trouble speaking her mind. Rather than using a bullhorn, Barbara wears her compassion for social justice on her pastel sleeve.

The bulwark for much of this compassion was her Southern Baptist faith, which consistently manifested in her career, within her family, and in her work as a Guardian Ad Litem (GAL). Barbara shared with me one experience during her more than twenty-year tenure as a GAL. She was assigned a little boy around nine or ten years old. He had been neglected by both of his intellectually challenged, low-functioning parents and was sexually abused by his father. Social Services found him wandering the streets and wanted the courts to place him in a group home. Barbara, knowing this would not be in the boy's best interests, persuaded the judge on the case to reject this plan. The judge turned to Barbara and said, "Okay, you've convinced me. I now leave it up to you to find a suitable arrangement for this young man." If the judge only knew how right she was to choose this direction. In no time, Barbara found a specialized foster care home with an older couple. The young man thrived with this couple, remaining until after his eighteenth birthday.

Barbara hails from Banner Elk in the mountains of North Carolina. Her roots there run quite deep. She is the youngest of thirty-seven first cousins in an extended family of historically meager means. This was, and is, the reality for most people in hardscrabble Appalachia. In Barbara's words, "We were a close-knit mountain family that loved each other fiercely. You messed with one of us, you messed with us all. It didn't matter if it was a fourth cousin twice removed; if we were kin, it counted." This was especially evident with her dad's death when Barbara was fifteen. Barbara and her mom carried forth, surrounded by the love and care of this indomitable clan.

It came to pass a few years later that Barbara left the mountains to get her degrees, marry Zeno, work and engage her passions in and out of the home, raise her girls, and eventually dote on her grandchildren. Much of this activity occurred down among the flatlanders in Apex, a suburb of Raleigh, the capital of North Carolina. Barbara and Zeno now have been married for more than fifty years. They are a true team. They have a rhythm and shared course that has helped shape the character and beauty of their family.

After Barbara and Zeno both retired, the open road beckoned, and they heeded the call. They set off in their RV to spend time in New Mexico with their youngest daughter, son-in-law, and three grandchildren. Back home now, Barbara and Zeno have both settled in nicely to the cadence of their lives at this time. Aside from enjoying his wife's company, Zeno spends time in his workshop, building furniture for their daughters and grandkids. Among other activities, Barbara engages herself with reading and writing, some of which is in pursuit of exorcising unsettled spirits.

This was where Barbara and I reconnected.

We crossed paths again when she invited me to join a Sympara writing group. The group was composed of folks in the second half of life, exploring themes salient to this time and our experiences. During one week in particular, our writing prompt was about the place of conflict in our lives. In Barbara's essay, she was working through a sense of the severing of her family roots. Much of her family remained in the insular environs of Appalachia. There is something visually, as well as metaphorically, striking about this characterization: a family embedded for generations in the valley of the titanic hills. Barbara's experience of family fissure resembled much of the time and environment in the larger country—fault lines along sociopolitical strata, identities of race and class coming into active strife. A number of her Appalachian kin were given to more strident, conservative mores, much in keeping with the greater ethos of this region of the state.

Barbara deeply loves her family. That they could hold such opposing views and values is painful to her. "My roots have been injured, and my identity dimmed. I am different now and believe different things," she stated in her essay. Despite this realization, Barbara is still drawn to the place and people of her blood. Indeed, Barbara and Zeno now spend a good bit of their time toggling between their homes in Apex and Banner Elk.

Underneath any blight, any root rot, or injury, there are still core values of care, determination, and dedication. And of love. Barbara accepts she cannot understand all their motivations but chooses to believe her kin are doing the best they can. Unlike the Shel Silverstein book, wherein the boy used the tree for his own self-serving ends, Barbara has cut herself away from the diseased parts of this family tree. She still holds the DNA, the life-giving core values, and she has planted her cutting (herself) with care and discernment, growing heart-shaped roots to carry forward in her family and community.

★★★

A portion of the Cherokee creation story:

> At first, the earth was flat and soft and wet. The animals of the sky were anxious to get down, and they sent out different birds to see if it was yet dry, but there was no place to alight. So, the birds came back to Galun'lati. Then, at last, it seemed to be time again, so they sent out Buzzard; they told him to go and make ready for them. This was the Great Buzzard, the father of all the buzzards we see now. He flew all over the earth, low down near the ground, and it was still soft.
>
> When he reached the Cherokee country, he was very tired; his wings began to flap and strike the ground. Wherever they struck the earth, there was a valley; whenever the wings turned upward again, there was a mountain. When the animals above saw this, they were afraid the whole world would be mountains, so they called him back, but the Cherokee country remains full of mountains to this day.[14]

★★★

Thermals
The sky is rife with my friends this morning.
Black and turkey vultures, gangly and oafish on the ground,
Yet these silent, majestic creatures
Carry grace and duty on the winds.
Maligned and cursed, they attend to their assigned roles
With singular sobriety.
No call for reward or thanks.
The Cherokee see the vulture as the winged Creator
Of the mountains and valleys.
Great wings beating the ground
Giving dimension to Life.
Depth and length
Depth and length
Long before our allotted time is called

We stare down into the valley
Where the wake is gathered.
We are transfixed in our disdain for the other.
We cherish our wounds like the great beast
Cradles the glass-housed rose
Dropping freedom with each felled petal.
Is it time?
No, it is not yet time.
What time is it?
There is no time, only flight.
Any religion that lays claim beyond mystery
Disrespects Life.
Would that we were like the red ones
Eating our necrotic fears.
Would that we were like the black ones
Gliding on thermals in sacred, sated peace.
Grace and lift.
Duty and purpose, ease and fill,
Depth and length.

★★★

My first record player was an early-1970s basic model from the Sears Roebuck catalog. I quickly amassed quite a collection of 45s and a handful of albums and spent countless hours lying on the floor in my bedroom with an ear pressed to the built-in speaker in the front base. I became adept at gently placing the tonearm and accompanying stylus on the preferred album track and listening to my favorite song du jour over and over. For a time, that favorite song was "Indian Reservation," a 1971 chart-topper about the sordid plight of the Cherokee by Paul Revere and the Raiders.

Common problems in those days would be a dreaded nick or scratch on the record's surface or an accumulation of dust or dirt, causing the needle to bump backward into the previous groove upon each revolution of the turntable. Skipping or getting stuck were common terms for this interminable annoyance. Sometimes, I could tape a penny to the tonearm to help the stylus soldier through with the added weight. My record player was one of my earliest anchors in the latest and last home of my childhood.

After several moves over my first eight years of life, my family finally settled in Oak Ridge, North Carolina, a rural community in the rolling Piedmont hills. My dad was from nearby Greensboro, and his mom's Irish family was several generations deep in the Great Smoky Mountains of western North Carolina. We spent many summer nights visiting our mountain kin in Andrews, a rural community south of Bryson City and Cherokee. We'd go primitive camping by what the locals called "Lake Chogie." The proper name for the lake is "Nantahala," which is a Cherokee word meaning "land of the noonday sun." This was fitting for the Nantahala Gorge, where the sun only reached the valley floor at midday. We'd pitch our heavy, olive-green canvas tent just off State Road 1457. This road was more of a meandering dirt path my dad's dad had helped build as part of the Civilian Conservation Corps (CCC) in the 1930s.

Coming from an already-meager background, my grandfather joined the CCC as an opportunity to climb up from the pummeling of the Great Depression. It was there, in western North Carolina, where he met my grandmother, the youngest and only daughter, following three brothers, of the Hogan clan.

In Oak Ridge, among other well-worn topics my friends and I had bandied about, we proudly proclaimed our respective ethnic heritages—that is to say, our White European ancestry. For many of us, our families were far enough along in generations residing in the United States, intermingling and intermarrying, as it were, with persons from other backgrounds, we would list off several countries of origin. Whether accurate or not, it was common to hear the ratio breakdowns: "I'm twenty-five percent English, thirty-three percent German," and so forth. While the math didn't always add up, it was safest to stay in Western Europe in these exchanges lest you be singled out for ridicule.

One exception was to claim Native American heritage. There was a mystique, a romantic aura, to being a member of the people of the land. The thoroughly whitewashed (painful pun intended) view of the Native Americans we read about in our fourth-grade North Carolina history class filled most of us with a longing to belong. At that time, we had little understanding of the horrific treatment of the Natives at the hands of a United States government comprised mostly of European immigrants and of the disrespect of cultural appropriation.

Within my own family, I had often heard from my dad that we had a small percentage of Cherokee heritage. This seemed highly plausible, given my grandmother's people had settled in Andrews in and adjacent to where many of the remnants of the Eastern band of the Cherokee Nation had lived. The remaining Cherokee successfully evaded President Jackson's forced migration to Oklahoma during the engagement of the Indian Removal Act, aptly named the "Trail of Tears," in 1838–1839.[15] I had accepted this family lore at face-value for many years and used this cachet on occasion among my elementary classmates.

At some point in my early adult years, my brother Lee came across an old family photo of our supposed-Cherokee ancestor. In typical droll fashion, Lee's clipped response was, "She looks awfully Irish to me." It was then I sidled into a state of doubt about this facet of our family heritage until I decided to pursue genetic testing in my early fifties. While not the exclusive domain of Third-Agers, genealogy is an increasingly popular pursuit amongst seniors.

In modern times, the field of genealogy got early traction in the late 1970s with the television broadcast of *Roots: The Saga of an American Family* by Alex Haley. His family story, tracing back to the African tribesman Kunta Kinte, inspired many to explore their own family histories. Mr. Haley phrased it well: "In all of us, there is a hunger, marrow deep, to know our heritage, to know who we are and where we came from. Without this enriching knowledge, there is a hollow yearning."[16] Knowing our heritage is indeed a seminal part of knowing ourselves. And while we can find value in this knowledge in our early adult lives, we often have other more predominant and present drivers to our sense of self, namely our careers and immediate family experiences. As we age, we tend to take a longer view of our place in the line of our foremothers and forefathers. This perspective can help focus us and shape our legacies, which we receive from the generations before us, and for which we care and offer to the ones who follow.

But what happens when we discover some part of our family story is untrue?

It was great fun to finally get my DNA results. Not surprising was the verification of our Irish line on my dad's side and our Polish and Czech heritage on Mom's. I had long heard of these histories. At this point, it was anticlimactic to get the confirmation that we, unlike Alex Haley, indeed had no Native American blood. We are 100 percent European. What *was* surprising was to see we have a fair percentage of Scandinavian ancestry. To my knowledge, this had never been considered or talked about within the family several generations back. A quick internet search reminded me how the Vikings, prodigious, peripatetic explorers and conquerors, had heavily intermingled in the nearby land of the Gaels, from whence came my people.

When I was relatively nascent in my career as a counselor, I was given to saying, "People will continue to tell their story until they feel sufficiently heard." By this, I was referring primarily to our stories of pain and strife. The idea being that, at a most fundamental level, our wounding experiences are ultimately about invalidation, about not being seen as an inherently worthwhile members of the human family. Once we felt heard, validated, we would no longer have the need to carry that particular mantle.

Over the arc of my career and my paralleling personal journey, I've come to see this experience is true … some of the time. Other times, like a few of my old records, people get stuck in their rupture stories. And the source of the stuck-ness is what's known in the therapeutic vernacular as "secondary gain." This basically means that individuals are reinforced, favorably responded to, when they tell their stories of mistreatment. This reinforcement is like sugar, one of the most addictive substances we know. So, they continue to tell these stories. And over time, these stories often become distorted, outsized, particularly when they become part of a larger family identity.

Sometimes, these stories stretch so much as to become contrived, co-opted, or outright stolen.

To be clear and respectful, there are authentic stories of retching abuse, trauma, and deprivation. It is most understandable for folks to get stuck in these stories. They overwhelm the psyche and its ability to form sufficient defenses and paths to resolution. It is not my position to place a qualitative value on any other person's experience. In certain times and settings, it is my call to offer feedback to another, to describe what I see and experience with their behaviors, their choices, and to express my concerns if the choices seem to be destructive to themselves or others. In other words, to shine the noonday sun all the way down to the valley floor.

Similar to Barbara's family story, my mountain kin were, at most, working class. I'm certain they endured the same hardships and hardscrabble living as much of rural Appalachia, continuing to this day. It was well-known around the time of the United States government's reparations to the descendants of various Native American tribes that there was the common experience of individuals attempting to "pass" as having Native American heritage by falsifying documents or having others "account" for their authenticity. I won't begin to judge the motives of our Irish "Cherokee" ancestor, though it seems likely she was one of the individuals seeking to gain fortune at the expense of the Natives. What is available to me at this time, several generations later, is further understanding of my family, its history, and my place therein. It wasn't about a Cherokee narrative. Rather, it was about my family's own close-to-the-earth living, sweeping cycles of scarcity, and, perhaps, occasional abundance, depending on one's perspective.

My father lived and modeled much of his life after this notion of scarcity imbued with an anxiety, wondering where the next meal may come from. This anxiety was more figurative than literal, but it did shape his ingenuity and resourceful nature. He received this passed-down family story on both parents' sides and carried it forward. The anxious weight of this story was too much for him to carry well, resulting in his extending another storyline within the family: alcoholism.

Given humanity's inherently subjective nature, and the thread of brokenness that lives and grows in one form or another throughout each family, there is an unavoidable darkness in every family's story. As we age and get to the time in our lives where we are inclined to do some personal historical review, having a better understanding of these distortions and offsets offers its own restoration, our own reparations to pass along to our children and theirs. Actually, it can be a gift to one's family—a penny on the tonearm to help heal the stuckness for the previous generations, and a plumb line for the subsequent generations to guide them in the creation and extension of their own and the family's continued narrative.

★★★

Life is naturally dirty. Our skin cells die and slough off in inestimable numbers. Life is naturally windy. The air pushes, a function of gases moving from high pressure to low and back again.

Imagine there is an ornate Victorian Tiffany lamp, replete with beveled curls and colors. A child approaches, wide-eyed, caught in the spell of its chromatic swirling ridges. The child smiles, sings, pirouettes, and leans in to drink all its majesty. "Grandma, come look!"

The wind carries the dust and deposits it onto the Tiffany lamp. Soon, the brightly colored glass becomes clouded, muddied even. The child loses interest, just goes and sits in the corner, bored.

The adults come in to clean the lamp, each with their smart devices, tapping and pecking and jockeying for a pane to test this theory and that. "I'll show you how to best restore this treasure to its original state," says one video found on the internet. Amidst the bustle, there are patches that show clear. Finally, someone blurts, "Eureka! I've found the answer!" And then the lamp is restored to its original, pristine state.

But then the winds come once more, and the motes drift and land like new-fallen snow, only not so white. The adults become distracted, lose interest in the process. Maybe one finds a great deal for a new Tiffany lamp online. They'll go outside and wait for the delivery.

Whilst they wait, the elder finds the child, and together they walk hand-in-hand back to the lamp. The two look at each other, eyebrows raised over curious frowns and shrugged shoulders. The elder pulls out two Q-tips, brown and frayed on the cotton ends. Nonetheless, she hands one to the child. They silently set about the work of clearing the colored panes. They begin with using the Q-tips to draw silly faces through the overlay of dust before moving on to a quickening game of Speed Racer, zooming in ever-widening, then narrowing, ovals. When the Q-tips become too gunky, the elder reaches into her pocket to pull out two more. The ones she gathers are even more dirty and disheveled. They just won't do the trick. With her pockets now empty, the elder looks to the child who grins and pulls two new ones out of his own pocket. They return to the quest at hand, rapt at both the process and the result. Soon, the space is brightened, colored light reaching out and mingling with the dust still dancing around the room.

Wisdom is often considered a function of advancing age; thus, it follows that elders are the founts of this gift. Actually, wisdom is neither bound to any age, nor is it a high correlate of context. "Out of the mouths of babes," we hear the psalmist say. An old English proverb proclaims, "There is no fool like an old fool."[17] The wisest among us may lose perspective given the right circumstances. Yet, each of us has an innate capacity for wisdom. Experience, it seems, is the necessary enzyme.

So, what does the elder have to offer to a society saturated with information? Wisdom?

Imparting wisdom is a non sequitur. Wisdom is an integration, ultimately an internal process. It can't be dispensed from the outside. The gift of the elder is experience. Together, with the elder and the subsequent generations, there can be the alchemy of wisdom. This is the work of legacy building.

T. S. Eliot offered this insight in the "Four Quartets":

We shall not cease from exploration
And the end of all our exploring
Will be to arrive where we started
And know the place for the first time.[18]

***

Legacy

While out looking for America
I pay heed to leaving marks on the trees
As I pass by.
I know the old tale of leaving bread crumbs
Will not serve my progeny.
Sometimes formula meets a hard, quick diminished return
And economies of scale have limited purchase.
Too many hungry beasts.
Too many storms cutting through the canopy above.
My only need is to recognize when I have moved in a circle,
Arriving more like Pooh than Eliot
In the same place I was before.
Unlike the Bear, whose sole purpose was honey,
I am in search of truffles, mint,
And the nectar of the honeysuckle flower.
Perhaps a dandelion clearing
To make my mother's wine.
My people have cleaved a path before me,
Giving me a quickened pace
But dulling my senses,
A drunkard slouched deep in well-worn, downy cushions.
My Blood's bone meal has replenished the earth,
Recompense for their stay,
Feeding the roots and shoots and buds
Of the Wood.
Often I have been distracted,
Too distracted by the scions and sallow bones of my people
Littered on the ground before me,

Stumping my toes on the very roots that at other times
Serve as risers for the steeper grades.
I have circled time and again.
Stepping on bone shards hurts every time.
So I look for the markings
And hope to make new ones,
Away from the shallow graves,
Deep in the lush green flora,
Newly trodden under my thick and calloused heels
Amidst the perfume of the virgin honeysuckle.

***

It has often been said that "there is nothing new under the sun" (Eccles. 1:9 NIV). In modern music, you can see three- or four-chord patterns repeated throughout many, if not most, songs. Even in things considered to be unique, we can see repeating patterns. Snowflakes are fractals, in which the microscopic crystals that make up the flake look much like the flake itself. Tree bark and broccoli buds or snowflakes and thumbprints, either common or unique, much of our experiences and environments are pattern-based. These patterns can and do have variance, but one needn't step too far back to see the resonant character.

My great-uncle Arvil Hogan was a member of the traditional band The Briarhoppers. The Charlotte, North Carolina radio station that first signed them, known as WBT, called it "hillbilly" music. They had a pretty good run for many decades, dating back to their humble beginnings in the Firestone textile mills of Gastonia, North Carolina in 1934. The Briarhoppers traveled the world, sharing their tight blend of high harmonies and old-time stringed instruments. In 1996, a few years before Arvil's death, they were honored at the North Carolina History Museum for their endemic contribution to the state's folkloric culture. I remember wandering through the band's exhibit before going into the auditorium for their performance. There was a rich collection of photos and varied memorabilia, detailing the band's life and music. Artifacts of a former time. I learned the name "briarhopper" was a reference to young folks leaving the farms of the

Appalachian Mountains to come down to the mill towns and big cities to find work.

I recently spoke with Kristin Scott Benson, Arvil's granddaughter. Kristin is an accomplished musician in her own right, still in the prime of her career. As I write this book, she is a five-time International Bluegrass Music Association's (IBMA) Banjo Player of the Year and the recipient of the 2018 Steve Martin Prize for Excellence in Banjo and Bluegrass Music. In addition to her solo work, she has been a member of the Grammy-nominated and two-time IBMA Entertainers of the Year group The Grascals. I was interested in hearing more about Kristin's relationship with her grandparents Arvil and Evelyn. She started with this inspired sense of legacy: "When I think about the marriage I want, I think of them. When I think about the parent I want to be, I think of them. When I think about the Christian I want to be, I think of them. I felt this way even when I was twelve years old."

Kristin described a picture hanging in her kitchen with the caption, "Laugh like Mema and Papa," and she shared an anecdote of her grandfather's assiduous faith, which included not cursing. "He loved his Atlanta Braves and loved and hated Bobby Cox. I never heard him curse. The closest he would come would be to say, 'Bobby Cox!' And that's when you knew he was frustrated with the game."

When Kristin chose to pursue music full-time after finishing at Belmont University, this decision was not met with enthusiasm by her father, who had just paid for four years of college. In the midst of this experience, Arvil said to her, "Kristin, when you're my age, the memories matter way more than the money. Do what makes you happy."

Arvil and Evelyn's clear-eyed, lifelong paths followed a simple and steady-tiered identity: a Christian first and foremost, then faithful spouse, devoted family member, and, for Arvil, musician. Kristin noted he never wanted to stop playing. Even as macular degeneration and hearing loss sought to deprive him of this core passion, he soldiered on. I remember watching in awe as eighty-five-year-old Arvil played on the History Museum stage alongside his longtime friends and bandmates, Whitey and David. Before each song, Whitey would lean in close and tell Arvil what song they'd play next. Arvil would then kick off the tune on his trusted mandolin, and Whitey and David would climb on board for the ride.

Kristin acknowledged that her grandparents set an otherworldly standard most of us mere mortals aspire to but come up short against time and again. I responded by framing this as a blessing and a challenge. A blessing to have their influence, guidance, and providence in her life, and a challenge to align with this model while not feeling like she hits the mark consistently. Kristin's comment reminded me of a popular saying attributed to Les Brown: "Shoot for the moon. Even if you miss it, you will land among the stars."[19]

Considering the converse, amongst countless "mere mortal" examples, I am reminded of one of my clients named Ellen and her struggles with her father. She and I sat down soon after his death. Ellen smiled and spoke lovingly about their relationship. In many respects, he was a fallen man, given to his history of heavy drinking and womanizing. Despite this, and the trials and storms they had weathered over pockets of her forty-six years, she spoke with respect for his spirit of intentionality and out-of-the-box choices. She told me about stumbling upon a framed certificate he had given her some years ago. He "bought" her a star, meaning the company had designated a star with her name.

"I know this is not officially sanctioned by NASA," she said, "but that doesn't matter. My dad always wanted to make me feel special. He never wanted to mail it in, so to speak. I look back now and realize that this mindset has evolved in me too. I find myself doing similar acts of originality with my kids. And I'm grateful, so very grateful to my dad for this."

In previous sessions, we had worked on the more tumultuous side of the relationship between Ellen and her father and the confusing and conflicting narrative of his hurtful choices abutting his care and love for her. There had been numerous times of discord and estrangement. One of the things that had helped her greatly was hearing from other family members who shared more family history—ways her father had been impacted by his parents, both for the good and the bad. This allowed her to not take some of her father's choices too personally.

During our session, she told me, "I feel more at peace, not letting my father have a free pass for some of the things that happened but more so being able to see his humanity. This helped me to see more of myself in him." Ellen smiled. "Mostly for the good." Her eyes then fixed on the floor. "Now that he has died, it's left to me to carry a part of him forward." She looked directly at me. "I know I don't need to wear his shoes, but mine are cut from the same leather remnant."

Legacy is a broad-spanning term. A person of means can bequeath a large legacy gift or endowment to their alma mater or most cherished cause. The legacy of war may be trauma or a lost generation. Most of us live somewhere between these two extremes, passing along to our loved ones treasured (to us) trinkets, habits of kindness, or perhaps resourcefulness. How do most of us consider our legacy as we move through the Third Age and into the Fourth (final) Age of our lives? I'm sure many of us focus on family and work. We want to raise our children to be good and successful, and we see ourselves somewhere within them. We want to achieve at work, as a means to provide a decent quality of life for ourselves and our family, or as a reflection and self-validation of our skills. A potential trap is comparing ourselves against some romanticized, mythical version of leaving for perpetuity a material product or act of grandeur. Legacy is the natural extension and conclusion of our identities—plural for each of us. We hope this usually bends us in the direction of our more essential character, rather than the more transient ones. If we are defined by an isolated event, more often than not, this comes from a terrible choice, a mistake not consistent with who we really are. Or a fortuitous moment of brilliance, also not consistent with our day-to-day character. These aside, how do we evaluate our legacy against our own unique standards? How do we craft a legacy that is both natural and intentional?

I love these lines from Ray Bradbury's *Fahrenheit 451*:

It doesn't matter what you do, he said, so long as you change something from the way it was before you touched it into something that's like you after you take your hands away. The difference between the man who just cuts lawns and a real gardener is in the touching, he said. The lawn-cutter might just as well not have been there at all; the gardener will be there a lifetime.[20]

The word *legacy* comes from the Latin word *legare*, meaning to send with a commission.[21] This root meaning suggests a shared enterprise. Neither you nor I are left to bear the full weight of what we hope to leave for our loved ones and community. Rather, we will send them our hopes and dreams with a commission, to share with their portion of the world—take our word, our deed, our creation—and extend it through themselves to fashion their own legacies moving forward. With that as our focus, we will surely land among the stars.

In 2003, Kristin was on the road, touring, when she got word Arvil was in the hospital, having suffered a roiling heart attack. It was deemed untreatable by the doctors. He would not have long to live. She was able to make it back to spend time with him before his death. While they were watching a Braves baseball game in the hospital, Arvil turned to her and said, "There's nothing left for me here. I am at peace."

Fractals are infinitely complex and yet simply self-similar. Each snowflake, replete with innumerable fractals, has a unique path to the ground, floating through different clouds with different temperatures and moisture levels. And yet, one needn't back up too far to see the resonant character.

Not all of us can do great things. But we can do small things with great love.
—MOTHER TERESA

Fusion food has really taken off in the past few decades. While searching for something new to try, I came across another in the growing cavalcade of amazing and unusual combinations: corn beef burritos with *pasilla* cheddar sauce. Who could've imagined a cuisine heavily dependent on potatoes, brines, and root-based vegetables, blending seamlessly with *especias picantes*?

I really enjoy my fusion friends Frank and Lauren. I met this couple many years ago at a Jungian retreat. Frank was an Irish priest in a former life, and Lauren was a Latina and adjunct dance professor at a nearby university. She is the more graceful swan to his sprightly cockatoo. He wears a constant impish grin under his thick, bespectacled eyebrows. Her amber visage is more demure, soft, and receiving. He came from a deep well of both staid and spiritual sustenance in his native family and land. She found light and green livery in the perpetual Ecuadorian summer of her youth.

They're both Third-Agers now. We recently had an in-depth conversation about their experience of being "care-ers," as Frank termed it, for his ailing Irish mother, leading up to her death. This protracted and increasingly grinding time was quickly followed by the unexpected twist of taking in Lauren's young grandson Miguel, due to her daughter's chronic struggles with substance abuse and mental illness. With enthusiasm, Lauren and Frank had taken him in two years prior. Their attitudes and pluck are quite impressive to me. Frank said Lauren has the patience of Job. Lauren then smiled and rubbed his arm, saying Frank was a good son to his mother and *da*—Irish slang for "dad"—to Miguel.

In the earlier essay introducing Sandra, the college president, I highlighted the importance of language and how we consider it, especially when it comes to labeling our sense of self, our identity. With insincere apologies to my Irish friend, who already amuses a simple person like me just by talking, it's all the more cute to hear certain words and the turned phrases Frank uses when wrapped in that animated brogue. Our conversation reminded me of how, in modern English, we have seemingly opposing words holding the same meaning: care*taker* and care*giver*. I'll step off of that platform for now but will keep one foot firmly planted on the word *care-er*.

The term *sandwich generation* was spawned in social work and gerontological circles to refer to the generation of caregivers (or caretakers), usually in their thirties, forties, or fifties who care for their aging parents while also supporting their own children. On her website sandwichgeneration.com, Carol Abaya, a nationally recognized expert on the sandwich generation, updated the phrasing to better capture the different looks of caring for family members today: "club sandwich," those typically in their forties, fifties, and sixties, sandwiched between caring for aging parents, adult children, and grandchildren, and "open-faced sandwich," referring to anyone else involved in eldercare.

We should add other deli metaphors for grandparents just raising grandchildren. Grandparents may be a substantial support to their busy adult children who, given any manner of circumstances, need help in caring for their own children. Perhaps for some, like my old neighbor Ron, the Vietnam veteran, we could call this experience the "soft taco," allowing for openness of involved parents at the top. For others, like Lauren and Frank, the need is all encompassing due to tragic circumstances by which the adult child is no longer able to care for their children. This feels more like a full wrap to me.

In the midst of the global pandemic, it was deeply sobering but not surprising to hear of the drop in United States average life expectancy by one year. The pandemic hit the elderly and communities of color disproportionately hard. Prior to the pandemic, the life expectancy trajectory was on a relatively consistent climb, allowing for a slight recent decline largely attributed to the opioid crisis, a pandemic in its own right. Overall, in 1950, the average life length was 68.14 years. Even with the COVID-19 and opioid pandemics, the average age was 78.99 by 2021. Across races, we've seen lower life expectancy rates, though still climbing among Native Americans and African Americans, while Asian and Hispanic folks have the highest rates. Some projections from the Centers for Disease Control and Prevention and the United States Department of Commerce show further gains of up to six years by the year 2160.[22]

Pandemics notwithstanding, thanks to numerous modern medical and nutritional advances, many of us still have our parents with us. Within this paradigm, for some of us, there may be the blessing of having financial resources and the time to respond to their needs. And the gift of less complicated moments together. For others, it could be seen as the challenge, or tax, on our material and emotional resources. Parents on meager, fixed incomes still requiring time and care. Unresolved and strident relationships. Each of us has a different story. This would be an important time to remember our essential charge of attending to, of cultivating and nurturing, our own support systems to keep our reserves well-stocked, to manage the loving and *caring* tasks at hand.

To this end, I'd like to offer a new term for the experience of caring: *careliver*. Perhaps the folks at Merriam-Webster will take note and reach out to me?

My mom Antoinette Mary Preiss, who went by "Toni," was the picture of health, save for a bout with breast cancer when she was in her mid-fifties. She was vegetarian, took daily walks in nature with her dog, Fudge, attended Mass regularly, and immersed herself in a life of productive work and avocational pursuits in music and literature. By her early sixties, she was very independent and seemed to be the happiest I had ever known her to be. Her mother was a lifelong renegade, who could go from playful to snapping-turtle mad as quickly as commuters rolling through a subway turnstile. My grandmother's diet was quite poor. She would famously gobble up the thick layers of dingy white fat we would trim off our pork chops at dinner. She lived to be a few months shy of one hundred. All these variables fixed in my mind that my mom had sturdy genes and would be around for a long, long time.

A cruel twist that visits far too many families arrived in February of 2004, when my mom was just sixty-five years old. My sister Pam and I sat with our mom in the oncologist's consult room to hear the words "CNS Non-Hodgkin's Lymphoma." This is more aggressive than other forms of lymphoma. The physician uttered the dreaded words "terminal" and "estimated two years."

From there, Pam and I were instantly thrust into the dual roles of caretaking, both for our mother and our respective young children, alongside our full-time careers. For each of us to be carelivers, we needed to tag team, share responsibilities for Mom's care, give each other breaks, and also find some healthy diversions and additional supports. Tough to do given all the demands of the time and experiences. One of my outlets was playing music, including in the band at the church my family and I had been attending. For Pam, spending time in the care of her sprawling yard was, and is, a healthy contrast.

There was no illusion that our choices for careliving were going to significantly alter the arduous path we were on. It's speculative to consider how much more challenging and grinding our experiences with our mom's cancer and subsequent death would have been had we not at least one steady outlet and each other's support.

Frank and Lauren have done well with their care for Miguel. He is a thriving, happy young man wrapped in their loving attention. Supporting this whole new time in their careliving lives, Lauren and Frank have each other and a fusion of friends and activities. For many, life may follow a more linear and somewhat predictable path. For many others, the unexpected turns invite us to expand our palates.

Frank sent me a poem a few days after our conversation about careers. It's called "A Prayer for the Caregiver" by Bruce McIntyre, and I have been given permission to share it with you here—technically, on his website, he's given anyone permission to share as long as he's given the credit:

Unknown and often unnoticed, you are a hero nonetheless.
For your love, sacrificial, is God at his best.
You walk by faith in the darkness of the great unknown,
And your courage, even in weakness, gives life to your beloved.
You hold shaking hands and provide the ultimate care:
Your presence, the knowing that you are simply there.
You rise to face the giants of disease and despair,
It is your finest hour, though you may be unaware.
You are resilient, amazing and beauty unexcelled.
You are the caregiver, and you have done well![23]

★★★

Years
You are just as likely to laugh as to sigh
At the gaps in my user skill set.
Your tufts of patience are brokered upon the evening sky.
I'm new to your gala, your fiefdom.
Each rotation always new.
I have read your books, your manuals,
Your maps.
I'm endlessly researching you,
Following your antics on social media
Until I am formula weary.
Why did you mock the man in the paisley dress on your 80th?
It was his too, you know.
His grandchildren were just having some fun.
Perhaps you were too?
You did well in loosely embracing
The woman of color and dignity on her and your 109th.

A dashiki in regal reverence.
How many more turns will we each have with you?
The queue stretches and lists,
More diffident souls waiting to dance
Reading pamphlet primers while swaying
As your magnum opus vibrates on the thinning air.
Your indifference maddens me
But as I look around at the contrasting hues of gray,
The paper wasp hive to the glossy quicksilver,
I recognize in early moments
Your steady helm at 56,
Your serpentine countenance at 72.
You are the flight of the Great Horned Owl
From time immemorial.

Act as if what you do makes a difference. It does.
—WILLIAM JAMES

Among some aboriginal tribes in Australia, their native languages have limited capacity for comparatives and superlatives. For example, the words *good*, *better*, or *best* are simply labeled as *good*. Distance is measured as *near, far,* and *away*. This simplicity would save most of us a lot of trouble in our day-to-day interactions. Via constant comparisons, we get ourselves tangled in self-limiting beliefs or needless and harmful judgments and reductions of those around us. Of course, there is also quite a bit to be said for the benefit that comes from using these discerning adjectives. There are times when our safety or betterment are the direct result of keener differentiation of experiences and relationships. Whether or not we use comparatives and superlatives, what ultimately matters most is authenticity. This is true at any stage of our lives. It has particular relevance as we approach and move into the Third Age.

I was introduced to Steve by an old friend who was his work colleague for many years. I was quickly impressed. He is a man on a self-guided mission. He started early with a paper route at age ten. When he was fourteen, he began working at a skydiving center and then went on to earn his pilot's license at age twenty. After college, he moved into the workforce, eventually landing as a vice president for an international company. He and his wife Lorraine were meticulous planners and savers preparing for the post-career time, the time after their two daughters were out of school, married, and into their own careers. Steve's original thought was to retire and then pivot right back into a life of consulting. This felt most congruent to him. By most Western standards, Steve ranked high on the positive end of the comparative and superlative scale.

And then the accident happened.

Steve described the precursors leading up to the accident: a long flight back from a business trip to Germany and ignoring the jetlag to attend to the leaves that needed blowing in his yard and a daughter's yard. "I didn't stay properly hydrated," he said. That night, he got up to use the bathroom and passed out. He described his head as a bowling ball bouncing off the floor. What was originally deemed to be a concussion actually was a brain bleed that nearly killed him. Post-surgery and recovery, Steve had the opportunity to reevaluate his priorities. At fifty-nine years old, this cradle Catholic found a greater connection in his church community. He began singing in the choir and assuming the duties of changing the weekly message on the marquee in front of the church.

A lifelong tinkerer and self-taught musician, Steve began playing music at a local nursing home where his aunt was a resident. He continues to do this today, even two years after her death. He is active on an advisory council and the board of a local school and is a docent at the nearby Air Museum. He crafts wooden toys for his grandchildren. He helps care for his ninety-year-old father, his mother-in-law, and his developmentally disabled brother who's living with their father. He still works two days each week for the company he has been with for the past twenty-plus years. He has decided on a gradual descent into retirement, with the intention of eventually moving from Boston to Maine with Lorraine. They also have a condo equidistant between their two daughters and their respective families, thus, they will continue being supportive and doting grandparents.

Steve is now sixty-two years old. Even during and after a near-fatal accident, he has lived life fully, deeply, and with an overarching spirit of gratitude. Those who know him attest to each of these attributes.

Talking with Steve, I had two words circling in my mind: *ambition* and *humility*. On their face, these characteristics may seem somewhat opposing. Ambition can conjure images of a hard-charging, cutthroat, singular drive with little capacity for the needs of the other. To turn a few dramatic phrases, "You're only as good as your latest success," and, "Eat or be eaten." Humility, on the other hand, feels soft, diffuse, almost debasing. If we dive a bit deeper, we can find a different picture that sees a more natural joining for the attributes of these two words. Actually, both are clear, active processes. They both speak to the authentic fulfillment of who we are.

According to the *Oxford English Dictionary* (OED), the word *ambition*, as a noun, is "an earnest desire for some type of achievement or distinction and the willingness to strive for its attainment." As a verb, "to seek after earnestly, to aspire to."[24] At its best, ambition is an honoring of our inherent need and drive to be who we were genetically coded to be, alongside our familial and cultural sculpting. It speaks to the personal desire as well as the transcendent, seeking attainment for the greater good. Living into the fullness of this, notably in our Third-Age years, is an apt and right completion of our circle. There is no need for comparative or superlative, especially when we factor in any manner of increasing physical or cognitive impairment or decline for each of us. We are who we are at each stage of our lives.

In my research, I found two considered Latin sources for the word *humility*: 1) *humus*, meaning "earth" or "dirt," and 2) *humilis*, meaning "low."[25] These are similar but set the course for an important disparate in the English definition. The OED defines the word *humility* as "the quality of not thinking you are better than other people." And a second, "a modest or low view of one's own importance."[26] This is in keeping with the Latin *humilis*. I much prefer the *Merriam-Webster* definition: "freedom from pride or arrogance,"[27] which aligns with the Latin *humus*, read "grounded."[28] Where arrogance is about self-inflation, an airy state, humility is the literal and firm ground upon which we stand.

There is an important caution for those among us who are moving into the Third Age. We have spent many years investing and cultivating ourselves within our careers and families. To step away from this can unmoor us, leaving us to a loss of self. Despite what the Oxford folks have to say, this is not humility. This is uncertainty. Authentic humility requires us to explore and embrace our talents, skills, and successes. It just also requires us to do so within the perspective of gratitude and magnanimity. Paradoxically, this may be a rightful home of comparative and superlative.

We do need to strive for the balance between humility and ambition. By acknowledging our strengths and limitations, we recognize that either of these states of being can be corrupted. One can chase after ephemeral power and vainglory, discursive praise and accolades, and even offer mawkish modesty. But these are just that: corruptions of what is an essential component of each of our supremely unique and simultaneously ordinary lives. We cannot pursue a healthy sense of ourselves and our purpose at any stage in life if we seek to dress ourselves in inauthentic, bright-neon colors or stuff our true gifts behind the closet door.

The best marriage of ambition and humility recognizes that, while we are but specks of dust in the unfathomable universe, we are unique specks, contributing something that wasn't a part of the glorious whole before or since. Rumi, the Persian poet, said it succinctly: "You are not a drop in the ocean. You are the entire ocean in a drop."[29]

Rumi's words are good.

Steve had to reimagine himself after his accident. He had lost some of his previous capacity. This led to a new experience of community and connection. Had he not reevaluated his lot and made the determined effort to engage in new pursuits, he ran the high risk of atrophy and dissipation. Unfortunately, this is not uncommon among Third-Agers. Community and connection are natural products of our choices to pursue authenticity and fulfillment. We'll explore more directly some stories of these experiences in the next section, but first, one last necessary poem and essay for our consideration of identity and meaning for this time in our lives.

★★★

Tea
What does Life do when She is visited
By the blackest bird
And the palest steed?
She invites the guests in, of course.
The faint horse is an old relative of hers.
The crow, a fraternal twin.
The three sit and share tea,
Life adds a cube of sugar, perhaps two,
To hold the bitter aftertaste in check.
They reminisce, the mount standing taut
Honoring Life as she disrobes,
Leaving her bright colors
In a tussle on the ground.
Before the winged form comes to hover patiently behind,
Lifting the shawl, translucent yet opaque,
And placing it over her shoulders.
A matter of woolen cause?
Or a considered act of care
For the coming chill?

★★★

In the summer of 1993, my mom, my brother Lee, and I hiked up to the summit of Mount Le Conte in the Great Smoky Mountains to spend the weekend in one of the guest lodges there. Mount Le Conte, officially in Tennessee, actually straddles the border with North Carolina and, at 6,593 feet, has the highest inn for lodging in the Eastern United States. It is notable for having no transportation to the inn. All guests must hike up to the summit on one of five trails. Because of the lack of access, supplies are brought in via helicopter and llama pack trains.

In the great room of the main lodge, there are iconic black-and-white photos, circa 1925, of the Le Conte family sojourning up the mountain to establish the inn and lodges. In one photo, ripe for comedic license, the patriarch, Joseph Le Conte, is seen using a walking stick and traversing the uneven incline with his mother-in-law, facing backward, strapped to him in a ladder-back cane chair.

The five trails vary in distance, ascending elevation pitch, and degree of difficulty. In addition to ubiquitous scenic overlooks and verdant mountain passages, each trail has unique vistas and challenges, consisting of root-ribbed and boulder-blocked points along the rising and falling sections of the trails. We took the Alum Cave trail, which is the most popular and the shortest, just shy of five miles one way. It is also considered to be the most scenic among the five.

One fond memory among many for me was hiking out to one of the overlooks late one night with my brother. A full moon was our main source of light along the path. I used the hackneyed line when Lee commented about the black bears that called the Smoky Mountains home: "I don't need to outrun the bear. I only need to outrun you. I'll be just fine." A statement to be fairly debated, if truth be told.

We need to include a discussion of death and the dying process within the larger conversation of identity and meaning. It may feel a bit early to focus on death for a book that is celebrating and extolling the experiences of the Third Age. After all, for many, this is a time marked by relatively good health and changes in life circumstances that allow for engaging in new or latent pursuits. Many of us would like to keep considerations of death consigned to the final stage, the Fourth Age. And yet, as we draw closer to death, it can leech or jut into our thinking and calculus. This is often fueled by seeing the first few harbinger deaths of friends or family. These experiences speak to the coming time and rites in our own lives.

I spoke with a colleague of mine, Pippa, who worked at hospice and transitions agencies for ten years before shifting to private practice with an emphasis on bereavement work. She described her time at hospice as "walking emotionally along an increasingly difficult path with families." She contrasted this with her bereavement work over the past four to five years. "With bereavement, you meet them at their emotional low point and watch them rise and improve over time."

I checked my ideas with Pippa about meaning for folks approaching death and the related impact on purpose for their loved ones and caregivers. I was pushing for the idea of a greater depth of experience. She spoke more of the earthy, the practical, beyond direct and immediate caregiving: "For the loved ones, the consuming purpose of caregiving throughout the disease progression often leaves no room to make meaning during the dying process. And the ensuing void and loss manifests a lack of purpose for many. 'Why am I here?' they ask. They have a lot to integrate."

Pippa went on to emphasize the importance of helping to create hope during an organic process of shifting priorities. When the bereaved loved ones ask, "Who am I now?" this often signals the coming ascent, the forward movement because it orients to the work of identity. This is a predominant question for a person losing their spouse. "It was us. Now it's just me." It has similar application and implication for other loss relationships. For Third-Agers, this commonly includes the loss of a parent.

Regarding the dying person, I asked Pippa what makes for a good death. She acknowledged some attention to legacy and making amends but primarily talked about the importance of being heard, of being able to express their final wishes for the practical things like DNRs, living wills, and estate issues, as well as the symbolic things expressed in rites after the death. Arching over all this experience is the quality of relationships. Pippa described the clinical label: terminal agitation. This refers to a cluster of symptoms wherein the patient exhibits extreme restlessness, often trying to get out of bed, pulling out IVs and the like. Anecdotally, she noted that terminal agitation was, at times, predicted by a lack of spiritual connection and poor or discordant relationships amidst the dying person and other family members.

Ultimately, there is not one single path to arrive at the summit of our lives and the lives of our loved ones. As clinicians, we can consider what healthier routes are and how to be present with our clients as they make choices. For all of us, clinicians and laypersons alike, there is wisdom in the experiences of those who have gone before us. It is an important gift to our loved ones to not wait until these last moments to have these conversations and clarifications of our wishes. Our deaths should be consistent and consummate with our sense of self, our identity. I respect that one of our greatest hardwired fears is dying. Regrettably, this fear can overwhelm and distort who we are, or who we see our loved ones to be. All the more reason to try and walk the less-inclined switchbacks toward the final summit, as opposed to waiting until the last moment and standing at the base of an oppressive vertical cliff with no discernible way forward. Paths that are opened and maintained still have arduous parts. But they are a far cry from scaling cliff facings and pressing through thick scrub and carrying others who are strapped to our backs.

In "Tendrils"—the next section of this book—I'll share more of my own experience with my mother's death. My purpose was self-evident and clearly defined in that experience, resulting in a hard but healthy deepening of our relationship.

PART II
Tendrils

We've got this gift of love, but love is like a precious plant. You can't just accept it and leave it in the cupboard or just think it's going to get on by itself. You've got to keep watering it. You've got to really look after it and nurture it.
—JOHN LENNON

The natural world is replete with form and function, beauty often intertwining seamlessly with utility. In the natural world, nothing is wasted; everything has its aesthetic. Specific to plants, there are many that use tendrils. These specialized, curly-cue stems, often a light-green shade emblematic of young supple growth, are sturdy yet elastic. These qualities help keep the plant from being torn away from its support during a storm or some other forceful intrusion. Tendrils are responsive to touch and certain chemical factors. They attach to solid structures, helping the plant to grow, to climb toward the essential light. There are certainly times and ways we experience invasive, stubborn plants that do more harm, given our preferred human sensibilities, and are great challenges to remove from our lives. Clearing away these plants with their tendrils is hard but good work. However, the clematis, the passionflower, the mandevilla, and the trumpet vine are among many lovely examples of the natural world showing off and bringing us along for the joyous ride.

Most of us understand the necessity of connection. We are hardwired to be social beings, irrespective of where we fall on the introversion-extraversion continuum. Yes, the neighbor two doors down can make you apoplectic at times with their incessant leaf blower going at any hour of the day or night, and your sweet, Southern cousin can sucker punch you with one line and then bless your heart with the next. We've all been there, yet we just can't go it alone … at least, not well. We need sturdy, dependable frames of authentic relationships and healthy environments. Like tendrils, we each respond to touch and chemical factors.

★★★

Bounce
Balls bounce.
People do too.
I once saw a young man on the subway,
Unkempt and soiled,
Ping off of the annoyed stares
Of Gucci bags and Neiman Marcus boxes
Like a bullet sparking off an angled steel facade.

Shuttlecocks bounce,
Or maybe they flounce
Off whipped rackets,
Like a child suffering the swings
Of taunting classmates on the bus
Before darting down the three steps
And into the shielding arms of her waiting mother.

Kangaroos bounce.
Sometimes in a lazy cadence that says,
"I wonder what I should do today?"
The instincts of predator and prey
With a force and determination
That even for an herbivore,
Speaks of life on the outback

Tiggers bounce.
They're the best bouncers of all,
For their bouncing is fueled by unadulterated joy,
A happiness undeterred
Despite Eeyores' gloom,
Poohs' doddering,
And Piglets' fear.

I'm rubber, you're glue. Whatever you say bounces off me and sticks on you.
—UNKNOWN

A h, the trials and tribulations of elementary schoolyards, where the insults, mockery, and retorts were simple and the pecking order ephemeral, like a game of King of the Hill. This is not to dismiss the very real cumulative trauma absorbed by those who perpetually dwelled at the bottom of this social hierarchy. But the process was simple and transparent. Our young words and actions often elicited direct and immediate feedback.

When I was a child in elementary school, for four consecutive years in grades three through six, I wrote reports on my then-favorite animal: the dolphin. I still love dolphins, but over the years, many more lives have jockeyed for first-tier status in my taxonomic fan club. I remember going to the school library and pulling out those old *World Books* and *Encyclopedias Britannica*. These were some of the very few times I enjoyed doing school assignments—just ask my sister, Pam. Among other traits, I was enthralled by the dolphin's use of echolocation.

This fascination didn't hold a candle to my more recent discovery of Daniel Kish who used echolocation after his eyes had been removed at thirteen months due to retinal cancer. He learned to make palatal clicks with his tongue when he was still a child. He now trains other blind persons in the use of echolocation and in what he calls "Perceptual Mobility." This refers to the use of any of the non-visual senses to engage and extend a visually impaired person's ability to function in their environment. The most striking example of his skill: he regularly rides a bike around town, even in rush-hour traffic.[30] Amazing!

Echolocation is the location and identification of objects by reflected sound, used by several kinds of animals, including dolphins and bats.[31] The image of bats sending out rapid-fire clicks or chirps to help them locate food and avoid slamming into tree trunks or getting tangled in your hair—sorry, I couldn't resist—got me thinking about Third-Agers. Strange, I know. As social beings who interact with our relational and material environments, we humans, of all ages and stripes, use a kind of figurative echolocation. We make choices of word and deed that go out from us and then return in the form of response (consequences). This is the most basic of psychology tenets and is invaluable for us in learning more about ourselves within the context of our larger surroundings. We send out many word and deed signals with stated or inferred messages, but for this moment, I will focus on one: *this is me.* We send this signal out, and it bounces off various people, trees, edifices, etc., then it comes back to us as either, *Yes! You are you, and I like it!* or, *Yes, you are you, and that's bland or even awful*, or, *No, you're not.*

For example: I send the signal out that I am a writer. I do this by writing books, posting related things on social media, and doing author visits. I've put this identity of mine out into the world. When my cherished readers come up to me at their local bookstore, smile, and say, "I *loved* your book. Better than anything I've ever read," well, then I am humbly affirmed. When the person sitting in the back row at my latest book talk raises their hand and blurts out, "I don't get it," I may be a bit chastened. Worse yet would be to not send out a signal or to send out a signal and have nothing, or no one, there for it to bounce off and return.

What do we do with these different responses? How adroit are we with respect to our perceptions of these responses?

It's common to hear Third-Agers say, "When I was younger, I used to care too much about what others thought of me. Life is so much easier now that I'm older and don't care." It intrigues me to follow the context that elicits these pronouncements. At times, there is a congruence, a true sense of peace accompanying this statement. Other times, there is a subtle air of resignation, contradicting these very words.

In psychology, we talk of internal LOC (locus of control) and external LOC. These two phenomena situate the source of our sense of self. The greater the internal LOC, the more impervious we are to outside influence. In the words of the inimitable Popeye the Sailor Man, "I yam what I yam, and dat's all what I yam."[32] The greater the external LOC, the more we are shaped and driven by the forces outside us. In truth, the high majority of us have some blending, pliable ratio of these two perspectives. There have been studies that show the development of a greater internal LOC with age, but other studies have been more ambiguous. I think a good, informal, and honest perspective check for each of us would be to simply ask, "At this time, how do I feel about others' opinions of me?"

If I were to write a school report on dolphins today, sadly, I would have to include a growing phenomenon of aging dolphins being trapped in fishing nets or beached. Research suggests this arises from dolphins being deaf and, thus, not being able to echolocate. This deafness may be tied to excess shipping noise or side effects from antibiotics flushed into the sea with wastewater. All sentient beings need some ongoing form of echolocation to survive and thrive throughout their lives. We Third-Agers need to take care to not become deaf to our world.

The quests of identity and purpose are lifelong. Even for the more essential aspects of ourselves that have sustained throughout most or all our lives, we have to learn anew what these may mean in new environments and times. In the Third Age, this can be a more vulnerable juncture. We are sending out signals into these new waters. We may have read about these waters, or seen a picture or two, or talked to others who have gone before us and who now inhabit this very space, but it is new territory for us. It is vitally important we take the time to consider which signals we are sending out into the world and how and what we do with the responses.

★★★

Homegrown Tomato
A crimson Beefsteak or Big Boy
Carries in its plump womb
The deep red energy of summer
Ready to release and spread

The sweetness of sunlight
Open space and memories
In the worn hearts of old childhood friends
On weathered front porch swings

The firmness of Shasta blooms
Petaled freedom reborn or renewed
Organic growth gained
Through coarse and dusty foliage

The meaty fruit of a child's baseball game
The dogged intention of life
As she stands on third waving to Mom,
Determined to make it home

The juice of an afternoon rainstorm
A mild musk lingering on the air
And in my mouth before the subtle, tart cleanse
Tells me I will know love once more.

Through consciousness, our minds have the power to change our planet and ourselves. It is time we heed the wisdom of the ancient indigenous people and channel our consciousness and spirit to tend the garden and not destroy it.
—BRUCE LIPTON

Rhonda and her husband Sam arrived in my office six months after Sam retired. They have been married for thirty-five years. They both had successful and fulfilling careers and relished—and, at times, survived—raising their two children who now have their own young families. Rhonda, steadfast and sensible, retired ten years ago. She spoke through her piercing blue eyes and platinum ringlet bangs of the unexpected bumps in the transition that eventually settled in nicely to meaningful involvement with her church and civic activities. More recently, she has taken a greater interest in cooking beyond the basic staples approach that was a better fit with a busy work and family life. She's come to love researching home remedies, especially using the various herbs from her garden—which have the advantage of her professional acumen.

Rhonda spent the bulk of her career working as an agricultural extension agent for a nearby county. She regularly advised residents on soil preparation, the best nutrients for their yards and gardens, how to manage pests and blight, and even how to invite healthy critters to join in the work. She spoke of worm bins, compost, cover crops, soil aeration, and constantly cycling nutrients to keep things fertile.

Ironically, to Rhonda's occasional embarrassment, regarding her own yard, this was a case of the cobbler's children having no shoes.

Before retiring, Rhonda acknowledged not always having the vigor and attention for repelling the pesky crabgrass or for regular and healthy pruning of her boisterous butterfly bushes. And she had no herb or vegetable garden to speak of beyond the occasional potted tomato plants. Since retirement, however, she has turned her attention to this passable but far-from-thriving backyard. She's even added several raised garden beds. And her time and intention have paid off well. She's quick to show pictures on her phone of her own bounteous garden. Her renewed and favorite saying: "A healthy garden is built on healthy soil." All these engagements aligned well for Rhonda. They filled her days at a comfortable pace.

And then, last year, Sam retired from IBM. For the whole of his professional life, he'd worn the preoccupied-programmer pants well. Head buried in his computer, he was subsumed in the technical matters of the day. But now he was retired. No more 9 a.m. to 5 p.m. grind. While this new phase was expected, and they'd had some discussions, they admitted to not planning thoroughly for the transition. Sam stumbled off the ledge.

Rhonda stated, "I love my husband dearly, but there are days when I just wish he'd go fly a kite. Literally. Find a new friend. Do something. For several hours. So I can do my own thing. I had this vague awareness of how we each have morphed over the years, but it was easy enough to stay busy and distracted and to not pay attention to those changes in him that really annoy or trouble me. He needs to find something to do rather than just follow me around or just sit in his recliner, watching that damn news."

In the preceding "Who Are You, Really?" section, we looked at the foundational roles identity and meaning are for card-carrying members of the Third-Age club. It is no small feat to explore and cultivate these twin constructs. And that's just when you consider *yourself.* What happens when you rotate ninety degrees and look at the person sitting in the Adirondack chair next to you? In this account, it's clear Sam has much work to do on his own process. But in this shared stage of the Third Age, what is Rhonda's role?

There is a new, wholly other, layer when one or both persons turn in the work ID badge for the final time. Over the past decade, several studies and surveys have shown a modest majority of people retire without any idea of how they will craft a life or adjust to retirement.[33] We've lived long enough to know relationships include hard work, grounds need periodic tilling and frequent care. We may have been hopeless romantics when we began lo those many years before, but we need to be wise and pragmatic romantics at this stage of life. The term *pragmatic romantic* may feel like an oxymoron, but I prefer to think of it as a healthy dialectic.

There are very real challenges unique to one or both partners having a significant shift in structure, routine, activities, and support systems. At a bare minimum, how do two people, accustomed to spending roughly four to six waking hours a day around each other, adjust to suddenly spending eight to fourteen hours together?

Gene D. Cohen, noted gerontologist and author of the seminal book *The Creative Age*, laid out a structure for pursuing meaningful relationships and activities to keep the soil of Third-Age couples healthy. He talked about engaging in new activities separately alone, separately with others, together alone, and together with others. This is a nice template to direct consideration and choices for experimenting, akin to the value of fallow fields and crop rotation.[34]

How well we navigate this foreign soil of recent retirement is also subject to how well we've prepared the ground in the time before the Third Age. Cohen's matrix is a healthy model at any age, albeit possibly more challenging when the majority of our waking hours are taken up with work and family obligations. Bruce Lipton, stem cell biologist and bestselling author of the intriguing book *The Biology of Belief*, describes how, day-to-day, we live 95 percent or more of our time semi-consciously ... in other words, on autopilot.[35] This works quite well and efficiently when we don't have to think about which turns to make on our daily drive to the gym, the same gym we've been going to for the past ten years. It's a greater test if our autopilot is about our communication patterns that may have subtly atrophied over time.

How tuned-in to your spouse are you after years of autopilot? Who is your spouse now? What are their current interests? Their passions? Their fears? Their irritations? Their hopes? Their joys?

Not sure?

Ask!

Practice in real time with your partner, even if the conversation is clunky and stuttering. Break molds. Foster new pathways. Find a class or seminar that may help start and move the conversation along. Passable gardens can be refreshed and reinvigorated. The fall harvest is upon us. It can still be beautiful and bounteous.

I'm happy to report Sam has taken up flying model airplanes, not kites. He's gotten into some impressive balsa kits worlds apart from the inexpensive Guillows Jetfire gliders kids bought at the dime store many years ago. And he and Rhonda have had several dinners at home with couples wherein Rhonda has practiced a smaller scale farm to table ambience, enlisting Sam to help in cutting herbs and pulling red potatoes.

★★★

Sniffer

Audrey is a world class sniffer,
Like how a Sherpa is a world class climber.
Her dedicated olfactory cells,
Mucus-covered cilia quivering, collecting
At 1,000 times the potency of her human friends.
How can this beagle be about
The business of playing with others
When her mind is engorged with florid bouquets?
Does she ever tire of the tangy torrent?

Her world can be so isolated.
But is she lonely?

Wait—
There she goes,
Her feral face flopping,
Randomly running after the pack
Of hounds and mixed breeds
At the dog park.

A deep sense of love and belonging is an irreducible need of all people.
We are biologically, cognitively, physically, and spiritually wired to love,
to be loved, and to belong. When those needs are not met, we don't function as
we were meant to. We break. We fall apart. We numb. We ache.
We hurt others. We get sick.

—BRENÉ BROWN

The Nepalese Sherpas have a remarkable capacity to live and thrive in the low-oxygen, high-altitude lands of the Himalayas. Owing to an advantageous genetic mutation, Sherpas have a unique physiology with thinner blood and less hemoglobin which allows them to function quite well with less oxygen. A study out of Cambridge University confirmed these findings. Andrew Murray, senior author of the study, concluded, "This shows that it's not how much oxygen you've got, it's what you do with it that counts."[36]

I have been chatting with my client John on the phone every Tuesday afternoon for several months now. He lives alone in a small ranch home in the heart of Raleigh, North Carolina. He retired three years ago at age sixty, having been downsized—what a terrible euphemism—and given a financial package from his employer. John worked in the hospitality business albeit behind the scenes, interacting very little with the greater public. Mostly, he kept to himself doing his same routine with little variability day in and day out. In the evenings, John was content to read Dean Koontz novels, binge-watch Netflix, and play video games.

Early in our conversations, John would regale me with stories of his past glories, his pride over successes at work, his relief at having resolved long-standing family conflicts or coming to peace with needing to let some go. He was grateful for finding sobriety twenty years earlier and accepting the bittersweet accounts of loves won and lost, including his divorce this year. And his cat Smokey. John dearly loved Smokey.

He was generally demonstrative and flamboyant in his tone, often randomly inserting into our conversations, "I'm so happy!" I sensed this was mostly true, but despite his repeated insistence, I occasionally heard a contrasting angst in the reverb of his voice. I knew, in time, he would share more about this rub.

We spoke again last week at our appointed time. Midway through our conversation, he paused and offered his "I'm so happy" refrain, but this time, it was even softer and more reflective. And then he added, "And yet, sometimes, I'm lonely too. Is it possible to be both at the same time?"

Understanding the context of his experience and not wanting to quibble over the clinical details, I answered, "Yes."

A 2019 study out of England showed that, in the previous year, one in five seniors had, on average, interacted with three or fewer individuals over the course of a week. And this was before the 2020 global pandemic effectively closed the world for months and months. According to the last United States Census, eleven million Third-Agers were living alone. While living alone does not inevitably lead to social isolation, it is certainly a predisposing factor.[37]

"Loneliness is the new smoking." This mantra has gained traction within the past few years, particularly driven by the rising correlation of the large cohort of aging boomers and the respective research linking deleterious health indicators and outcomes to loneliness.[38] As noted earlier, many Third-Agers retire before they are psychologically ready. John echoed this sentiment in lamenting the loss of connection and interactions he'd had while at work.

Related to this is the amplified effect of retiring when married or coupled and unexpectedly running into disruption and disconnection in this relationship. There is a line from the old Three Dog Night song "One" that talks about how two is the loneliest number since one. That feels rather apropos in this case. Thankfully, for Sam and Rhonda, their experience was more of a clunky transition rather than a concretized state. But there are many others, including John, for whom this was (or is) an established pattern, one that more and more often is leading to "gray divorce," the increasing trend of late-in-life divorces.[39]

To be fair, allowing for our human connection hardwiring, we are all calibrated differently somewhere along the introversion-extraversion continuum. Sure, there are a certain number of relational Sherpas among us, those who are truly happy with less human contact. But less is not zero. Sherpas do require oxygen to live. We, all of us, do require social connection to live. Our life experiences, planned and unplanned, give great shape to the quality of our connections, but there is no denying underlying genetic coding for these. Darwinism would frame this as survival of the fittest … species, or at least identified social group.

Sarah is not one of those relational Sherpas. She is more of an ambivert, enjoying her time alone but appreciating her need for connection and interaction, especially following her retirement from her state job as a biologist and an unexpected divorce after thirty-four years of marriage. These two life-defining events occurred within months of each other when she was seventy years old.

I met Sarah last year at a retreat in her new town, the quaint and beautiful Beaufort, North Carolina. Beaufort sits on the Pamlico Sound on the North Carolina Inner Banks. The town is known for its unassuming waterfront park and stately historic homes, shops, and restaurants, replete with flowers of riotous colors, draping over porch railing boxes. Standing sentinel in front of the homes are massive, gnarled, and sprawling live oaks and other virile hardwoods. Nature's grand finishing touch to this scene is the Spanish moss, clumped on branches and slightly listing in the morning sea breeze. Sarah has long loved the North Carolina coast and made the decision to move to Beaufort when the divorce was finalized. She saw this as her opportunity to cultivate a new life out of the hard transitions just past. Her three kids are grown with families of their own. One daughter lives in Baltimore, another in Charlotte—about a five-hour drive from Sarah—and her son lives in Raleigh, two-and-a-half hours away. Sarah likes the space to do her thing and the reasonable proximity to see her family.

During a break in the retreat seminars, I joined her for a walk on the boardwalk that sidled along the water. We stopped and looked out at the idyllic scene. The dark-green water undulated lazily, lapping both against the lower algae-covered posts of the boardwalk beneath our feet and also sixty or so yards out to the shore of a long, paralleling island where a lone, feral horse munched casually on sea oats.

Seeing the horse, Sarah surprised me by reciting a few lines from one of my favorite poems, "A Blessing" by James Wright. After my gushing over this, she repeated the line: "There is no loneliness like theirs."[40] She smiled wistfully and homed in on this feeling. I listened as she described failed, tepid efforts to connect in her new community, eventually leading to the feeling of being "dried up."

Asking a few questions, I sensed Sarah was understandably stuck in her perspective. I pointed to the water and asked, "You're a biologist. What do you know about the composition of this water?"

"Well, it's brackish, with more salinity than freshwater but not as much as seawater. It's rich with plant and animal life. Home to many species of young fish, crabs, oysters, and clams," she replied.

I thought about the life beneath the surface of the sound. "So, all of this abundant water, from which life can certainly thrive and derive sustenance. This life would not thrive as well in either fresh or saltwater exclusively?"

She shrugged and nodded. "Many would adapt, but they would need time."

"What are you doing with your time?" I asked.

"Mostly reading and feeling sorry for myself."

"Both good things, to a point. But not sufficient, as you know."

She pitched her eyebrows.

I went on to elaborate on the value of alone time and also, in a limited scope, the place for honoring one's sadness and loss. Sarah easily acknowledged her mixed nature, including ordinarily relishing time alone.

I then pivoted from the saltwater of her solitude to the freshwater of her time spent with others. We talked about how she might engage her interests to find a fit within the brackish waters of a volunteering opportunity. This led, I learned a few months later, to Sarah reading to folks at a nearby nursing home. This may seem cliché, but the substance of this experience couldn't be more meaningful. She sent me a happy-face-emoji-laden text with a picture of her intently peering at a copy of an Erma Bombeck book, with an older woman smiling, sitting next to her in a wheelchair.

Abraham Maslow was a seminal figure in psychology. He created his Hierarchy of Needs, which detailed the upward movement for individuals from the most basic requisite need of the essentials for survival, through safety and security, to emotional connection, esteem and respect, and, finally, the pinnacle of self-actualization. Maslow posited that an individual will always default to the lowest level of unmet need.[41]

With great respect for Dr. Maslow, while I agree with his idea that we will orient to the most primary, unmet needs first, I disagree with his order. Time and again, we see the behaviors of others, or ourselves, being driven by the need for true connection. We may even settle for tenuous or superficial belonging and work really hard to make ourselves believe it to be authentic. We will forgo the more traditional, basic needs of food, clothing, and shelter if it entails a relationship for which we assign the value of real connection. The overall gist is, we are better together than apart.

I've always been intrigued by the verified medical condition called "Failure to Thrive." Newborns who are not sufficiently touched, talked to, or, in general, interacted with are at an increased risk of poor or delayed growth or even having their organs shut down, with no discernible cause. We know of many accounts of couples who have been together for decades in a relatively healthy relationship. When one dies, the other, who, heretofore, was in unremarkable health, declines and dies in a short time span.[42] The colloquial phrase "died of a broken heart" has only recently found its way into the formal medical nomenclature. Takotsubo cardiomyopathy—a.k.a. "broken-heart syndrome"—is the medical condition wherein the heart, in response to a traumatic loss, can change shape. A lobe becomes distended, rendering it unable to pump very effectively. Some folks recover from this condition ... others do not.[43]

"Loneliness is the new smoking,"[44] remember? It took us some time to catch up to the grave health implications of smoking. But then again, we were working against a powerful tobacco lobby and a generations-deep, permissive public sentiment. There really is no comparable resistance when considering loneliness.

Whereas overall divorce rates in the United States are at a fifty-year low, the demographic with the highest, and climbing, rate of divorce is in the fifty-five to sixty-four-year-old age range.[45] Some folks are finding newfound freedom with the mantras "carpe diem" and *The Lion King*'s "hakuna matata" lighting their Third-Age path. This choice can be empowering and healthy. It was not fully so for John nor Sarah, although, John tried to convince himself otherwise. Social scientists will continue to delve into this to better understand the drivers for this newer phenomenon. It may take a while to understand the impact of the COVID-19 pandemic, but this "gray divorce" trend was showing itself prior to the global health crisis. Longer and healthier lives, greater—though, still not equal—economic independence for women, the attenuating stigma of divorce, and other variables may contribute to this pronounced experience. Nonetheless, whether an empowering, deflating, or mixed experience, this is a transition that needs intentional response and care. In spite of their physiological gift and advantage, Sherpas who lead expeditions up Mount Everest approach their craft with a sober respect every time. Loneliness, like the air we breathe, is not to be trifled with.

Life is short. It's up to you to make it sweet.
—SADIE DELANY

Sadie and Bessie, the Delany sisters, stepped into the greater public eye in 1993, when they were 103 and 101 years old, respectively. The book *Having Our Say*, written with Amy Hill Hearth, was the story of their remarkable lives. It was a huge success, bringing the revering spotlight of talk shows, radio interviews, and, eventually, a movie. They had already lived quiet, heroic lives, as was in keeping with the family's makeup. They were born in Virginia and raised in Raleigh, North Carolina, on the campus of St. Augustine's College, where their father Henry and mother Nanny both taught. Henry was born into slavery and became the first elected African American bishop of the Episcopal Church in the United States. Nanny, in addition to being an educator, birthed and raised ten children.

"Bessie was what we used to call a 'feeling' child; she was sensitive and emotional. She was quick to anger and very outspoken. Now I was a 'mama's child' and followed my mama around like a shadow. I always did what I was told. I was calm and agreeable," said Sadie.

In Bessie's words, "We were best friends from day one!"[46]

The sisters went on to stalwart careers and tireless civil rights advocacy. Sadie was a schoolteacher and the first African American to teach domestic science on the high school level in New York City. Bessie was a dentist, the second African American to practice dentistry in New York City. They survived many encounters with racism and sexism, relying greatly on each other and their family.

And neither one ever married.

After finishing their respective educations and establishing their careers, they moved in together in Harlem, New York. They migrated to the Bronx when it was still somewhat rural and eventually moved to Mount Vernon, New York, where they bought a house together and lived out the rest of their lives.

In the book, when asked about the secret to their longevity, they spoke of doing yoga every morning. Bessie then added, "Honey, we never married. We never had husbands to worry us to death!" That and, lightness aside, they also had supports and purposes with their careers and steadfast civil rights work.[47]

Betty Walker was hands down my favorite high school teacher. She had support and purpose too. She was never famous, save for the hundreds of young persons' lives she touched through her long career as a biology teacher. She was tough, cool, and dedicated, with a slight impish twinkle in her eye. Her steadying guidance for me lingered into my early college years in the form of letters we would send one another. Nothing of great depth or substance; we were just staying connected.

As I moved further into college life and my attention turned forward, I lost touch with Betty. I kept fond memories of my time in both of her biology classes, and when, on occasion, I was reminded of her, I saw her subtle smile with a hint of mystery but always a commitment to her charges, her students.

Then word came in 2017 that Betty had passed away. I reached out to another important pillar of my high school years: Linda Case-Reynolds. Linda was my world history teacher and National Honor Society advisor. In asking more about Betty, Linda told me, "She chose the single life and sometimes wondered what life might have been had she married. I am sure she remained in teaching because she was single, and hundreds of students reaped the benefit. Her contribution was gargantuan!"

While I didn't know more about her family background and personal life, it was clear she was well-respected and had a connected sense of family within her teaching peers. Over many years, with faculty, staff, and students, she had a deep well of kin and kith.

Third-Agers who are lifelong singles share an abundance of the same dynamics and issues, as do seniors who are married, widowed, or divorced. And yet, they do have a different lens, their experiences being shaped and colored by this unique perspective. Whether single by choice and constitution or through ill-fated circumstances, many of these folks, of necessity, over many years, have evolved a keener lifestyle of pursued interests and connections. Of course, the rest of us cannot replicate the whole of this perspective, and while there is no guarantee of becoming happy centenarians like the Delany sisters, we can learn from their presence and intention.

★★★

Salad days is a term that refers to times past and is often associated with a fond and longing look back to our days of youth.[48] To play off this idiom and cross it over into the literal, when I was a young teen, I wouldn't go near a salad. I was not open to the freshness of spinach and kale or the decadence of one of those beefsteak tomatoes. I was a sandwich man through and through. And when I say "sandwich," I mean no ordinary hero. I quickly perfected the art of the triple-decker bologna sandwich, deftly alternating the mayo and mustard on opposing sides of the, of course, white bread. No fresh produce, just processed meat parts and condiments. It wasn't until later my world was availed of the majesty of fresh vegetables.

Looking back to Frank and Lauren's story in the "Who Are You, Really?" section, we were introduced to Carol Abaya's work in coining the term *sandwich generation* and extensions on the theme to include *club sandwich*. This important work sought to identify the dynamics at play when individuals have to contend with expected or, more often, unexpected changes within their families. Either scenario can result in the needed care of parents, children, and perhaps grandchildren. The approach is often problem-solving in nature in the pursuit of mending family ruptures. There is another essential and generative angle from which to consider interactions across generational lines: intergenerational connectivity.

Tuck Kamin was a fellow member of the Sympara Writing Group referred to in the "Who Are You, Really?" section. He's had a long, distinguished career in advertising and image-consulting and is naturally gregarious and inviting, with full-bodied, dusty-gray locks and a wrinkle-free visage. His youthful spirit is befitting his worldview of the rightness of connections among many ages and backgrounds. From an early age in his small Southeast Texas hometown of Victoria, he was nurtured in the benefit of intergenerational relationships, notably by his grandmother. One example was her, in her late seventies, getting on the floor and playing marbles with young Tuck. He said, "My mother would say to her, 'Mom, act your age!' to which my grandmother would just wave her off."

Tuck's interest in intergenerational connectivity was later piqued on a visit to the San Juan Islands off the coast of Washington. He described the time he met a couple of super-agers. A super-ager is a person in their eighties or older, possessing the cognitive or physical functioning of someone decades younger.

"I was chatting with a lady," Tuck said, "active and animated, in her eighties. She tells me that her boyfriend is coming over. I soon see a Mercedes SUV pull up, and out pops this ninety-two-year-old man dressed in workout clothes. He sticks out his hand and says, 'How the hell are you?' I felt like I was on this *Island of Dr. Moreau*, ageless thing." He then added, "How is it that people who are older are enjoying full lives when I see people I've gone to school with that are older than their parents?" This experience further compelled Tuck to connect with age scientists across the United States to unpack and understand the psychology and practices of super-agers.

A few direct applications of Tuck's search included him writing his book *Design Your Age: What's Best About You Never Ages* and his work with the Age Circus. The Age Circus is a digital app that arose from the explosion of Zoom meetings as a medium for people to connect during the COVID-19 pandemic. Tuck recruited fraternity students at several universities to meet with seniors for virtual conversations of forty minutes or so. He described the results as magic and foresees a changing future wherein senior living will be demonstrably reconstructed. To wit, he illustrated the power of intergenerational settings and communities by citing the example of Humanitas Retirement Village, an intentional community near Amsterdam that brings in students to live for free with the stipulation of spending thirty hours each month interacting with the active senior residents. Similar communities have sprung up in places like Lyon, France and Cleveland, Ohio. Tuck references a bevy of research, showing the improved physical and psychological health markers within these environments.[49]

We see the majesty and grandeur of intergenerational connections in the natural world as well. In her remarkable memoir *Finding the Mother Tree*, Dr. Suzanne Simard, a research scientist at the University of British Columbia, laid out what is—but should not be—astonishing research that confirms the intergenerational and interspecies cooperation among trees the world over. Her research has been situated in Western Canada. Here, as in many places in the aftermath of clear cuts, big agribusiness, with the blessing of the British Columbia Ministry of Forests, has sought to plant large swaths of single-tree species in symmetrical lines. This is done for logistical and profit expedience with whichever species may be in economic vogue at the time.

As a needed foil to this practice, Simard has shown the vast underground network between older "mother" trees and their direct offspring and cousins and completely nonrelated other species and organisms. Fast-growing birches send nutrients in the spring and summer seasons to slower-growing firs. In the winter, the goods go the opposite direction with the evergreens sending carbon and sugars to the birches. Mother trees send important chemical messages about environmental dangers like drought and bug infestations to the younger trees. The whole delivery of this vital, life-serving enterprise is handled via networks of mycorrhizal fungi. The net sum of Simard's research is that the healthiest and most economically advantageous arrangement is to support biodiversity, with planned plantings of varied tree species and ancillary undergrowth shrubs and plants. Just as important, the cultivating and harvesting of trees should allow for retaining some of the mother trees in the service of the overall health of all the trees.[50]

In traditional terms, we see grandparents playing with small grandchildren. What happens as the children become teens or move into early adulthood? Yes, interests diverge and, in some respects, don't fit together well. This is often where we see an erosion of the connections and interactions or a shift to an important supportive posture that nonetheless may be less active and facilitating. As evidenced in Tuck's travels and explorations, there is still room for exploring mutual interests and capacities and cultivating appreciation for those divergent interests. Akin to our neighbors on the flora side of life, we need the involvement with different generations, both inside and outside our families. This cross-breeding creates new and sturdy communal roots that serve us all well through times of plenty and want.

★★★

Bridges
I stand at my friendless window,
Thoughts of him driving the same route
As I stare out over the Foxglove,
Untiring in its fight through the broken rock and rebar.
With the fretful linger of a Chopin Nocturne,
I sit and wait for the winter.

While Peter Pan draws circles in the hard red dirt
With a calloused bloody finger,
Many charred bridges still have solid girders
Waiting to be awoken and walked upon,
To be reminded of their joy and function,
To be washed and sealed in loving linseed oil.

Too common is the shame,
Too poetic is the desolation
That they remain untrodden.

★★★

I recently watched a remarkable film about a man named Alvin Straight. He was a reclusive, blue-collar family man and veteran of both World War II and the Korean War. He was retired and living in Iowa when in June of 1994, he received word that his older brother Henry had suffered a stroke. At the age of seventy-three, Alvin—in failing health from diabetes, emphysema, and arthritis, as well as having such poor eyesight, he could not pass the driver's license test—decided to ride his aged, red lawn tractor two hundred forty miles from his home in Laurens, Iowa, to see his eighty-year-old brother living across the Mississippi River in Blue River, Wisconsin. His story, parlayed into the motion picture *The Straight Story*, certainly accounted for a unique expression of the iconic "adventures on the road" theme that captures the fancy and imagination of so many of us.

Alvin and his brother had been estranged or, at least, had fallen away from contact and connection over many years. Early in the movie, Richard Farnsworth, who played Alvin and was nominated for a Best Actor Academy Award, said, "Well, I can't imagine anything good about being blind and lame at the same time, but still, at my age, I've seen about all that life has to dish out. I know to separate the wheat from the chaff and let the small stuff fall away." Over the course of six weeks and at a top speed of five miles per hour, Alvin rebuilt and crossed the bridge back into his brother's life.[51]

Unsurprisingly, the process was uneven and challenging. He hadn't made it twenty-five miles when the old machine gave up the ghost. He was towed back to town, and, unbowed, he bought a 1966 John Deere 110 riding mower, said "goodbye" to his wife and daughter again, and set off once more, hauling a ten-foot trailer with supplies and extra gasoline behind. A few more mechanical failures, perilous traffic, financial strains, and heavy rains—all of these were cuts and scrapes that colored and refined both the trip and the greater process.[52]

As a rambunctious child, I could have been a perfect casting for an antiseptic spray commercial. Taking numerous bike spills on the gravel road in front of our house or scraping myself when tumbling out of one of the large oak trees in the backyard, I seemed to have a standing collection of cuts and scrapes. As with the child in the commercial, I was loath to have my wound cleaned of the gravel or bark flecks and dirt and then sprayed with an unexpectedly soothing balm. I would much prefer to stay with the known quantity of pain than to increase it, even if that meant quicker and better healing.

Fast forward a couple of decades. After many years of distance-running and playing basketball, my right knee told me it was time to properly tend to it with arthroscopic surgery. Being the curious person I am, I decided to have a local (rather than general) anesthesia, so I could watch the procedure on a nearby monitor. The surgeon explained what he was doing throughout the operation. The last thing he did, after suturing a long tear in my meniscus, was take what looked like a cheese grater and vigorously scruff up the impacted area. He noted that this aggressive act, this conflict, would stimulate the healing process.

I have spent the length of my life in search of peace, and indeed, I have found it.

In moments.

In periods of time.

And then, each time the peace promptly left, I ardently searched for its return. The personal and professional work of my life is learning to dance with conflict. I am finding the more adept and at ease I become in this dance, strangely, the greater the peace I experience. Summarily, this feels like a direct manifestation of the Buddhist Four Noble Truths in that the acceptance of all things leads to peace.[53]

One of the earliest accounts in the Torah and the Bible is that of Adam and Eve. As the story goes in the book of Genesis, the pair lived a serene existence before being cast out of Peace. This is the conflict that we, their heirs, continue to grapple with today. But if we go back and consider the account more closely, Adam and Eve were already in a state of disconnection before they were expelled from the garden.

They were distressed *before* being approached by God. Being cast out (read: conflict) was the unavoidable result of their inherently subjective human nature. And the catalyst to their healing. The conflict was, and is, the necessary ingredient for the path to wholeness. The poison is the cure, oddly enough.

Conflict is as natural as the moon's gravitational pull on the ocean's tides, the tidal force, pushing and pulling, creating and sustaining the base of the entire world's harmonious ecosystem. It seems equally natural for a majority of us to avoid conflict in one form or another. I say "seems equally natural" because avoiding conflict is more often *not* natural. It's learned. What's not natural is the state of sustained disconnection.

In accepting conflict, we all would do well to remember that anger and conflict are two completely different experiences, albeit ones that are highly frequent bedmates. Conflict and anger are both voluble, active energies. But anger most often has an unhealthy fear as its wellspring. For the conflict that is an inherent component of life, unhealthy fear has no place in the calculus. Peace, on the other hand, while also voluble, is a receptive energy. Peace is a state of resolution, a state of acceptance that requires conflict, just as light requires darkness. Each defines the other.

So I come to find that the real steps I need to master in my dance with conflict involve greater understanding of my fear and anger. This is true for many of us, as stories of family and friend ruptures and degradation are too common for many Third-Agers. There are times and ways it is truly necessary, for emotional safety and health, to sever toxic ties. If we deem this path to be the right and necessary one, we embark on a different journey, one of grieving and coming to authentic acceptance of the loss in our lives. However, too often for many of us, the burned bridges really do retain solid foundations despite their outward, charred appearances. It is then more a function of pride, shame, inertia, or fear that we invest untold amounts of time and energy in maintaining animus with the other. Or worse, we fall asleep in the poppy fields around the Land of Oz, dulling our lives with meaningless pablum or harmful vices that deter us from getting to Kansas.

Alcoholics Anonymous (AA) is a well-established and lifesaving milieu for millions of persons across the globe. The basis for AA is the Twelve Steps, each step being a statement and a directive at the same time. I've found the Twelve Steps to be a healthy structure for all of us, addicts and non-addicts alike. The fourth step speaks of the need to make a "fearless moral inventory," an examination of all the ways we have caused harm to ourselves and others. Step eight extends this with the making of a list of individuals whom we've harmed along with an expression of willingness to make amends to them. And then step nine goes to the action of making direct amends, "except when doing so would cause injury to them or others."[54] This can be a frighteningly tall order for most of us. Unlike many alcoholics engaging in the ongoing work of sobriety, and who have often weathered dramatic, searing ruptures in relationships, most of us are patchwork quilts of defenses to slights—given and received—we've sewn in along the way. We believe our quilts to be sturdy enough as they are. To go about the work of removing various defensive squares within the body of the blanket would be unduly disruptive and compromising to our stability. And so, we live out our days, protecting our wounds like children in pain-relief commercials, living truncated lives given to the loss of connection(s) that would bring more depth and richness to our—and our estranged loved ones'—worlds.

I'm not sure what compelled Alvin Straight in *The Straight Story* to drive a John Deere riding mower across an atrophied and charred bridge to reconnect with his brother Henry. The movie most certainly took some license in scripting motivation and dialogue. Following the success of the film, there were many requests of Alvin for interviews and guest appearances on late-night talk shows. He turned them all down save for one with Paul Harvey. What we do know is a blue collar man, a veteran of two wars, a father of twelve children—only seven of whom survived beyond infancy—a widower after forty years who remarried and helped care for his adult daughter with developmental delays decided, despite appreciable physical limitations, to find some peace.

★★★

Verdant Groves

I know you.
I've seen you many times
In my dew-streaked morning mirror.
This is no Narcissus myth.
We share sustenance and breath
As if conjoined, one body, one spirit.
You touch me in memory,
In the grocery aisle, reaching for the granola.
In real time, at the corner table in the coffee shop,
You, sipping hot chocolate through heavy cream.
I smell you in the cotton fibers
Over my mottled shoulders
And hear you in the throbbing refrain
Of tree frogs in the shimmering, summer leaves.
In Southeast Maine,
We stroll through verdant groves
Taking in comely creatures
Whispering words of wonder
At the rightness of our union.
In and out of time and space,
I know you.
I've always known you.

★★★

Michael Douglas starred as Sandy, an aged acting coach, in the TV show *The Kominsky Method*. Over three seasons, the show peered into the themes and experiences of Third-Agers with humor and pathos. There is a scene where Sandy and his lone middle-aged student Lisa, a recent divorcée played by Nancy Travis, have a romp in the sack.

Following the sex, Lisa compliments Sandy on his performance and presumes he used medication to help him. Sandy feigns an earnest, implied denial by listing off a handful of prescriptions he takes for various other medical conditions before pausing and adding the last med: twenty milligrams of tadalafil (Cialis).[55]

There is a growing body of research and literature that shows a shift for older adults in the direction of having more and more satisfying sex. Historically, prevailing societal norms and limited public dialogue likely contributed to lower numbers—this along with greater physical limitations. As people are living healthier lives into their later years and have the benefit of advancing medical support, as well as more agency for healthy dialogue with their partners, it's not surprising to see these shifting statistics. A healthy sex life is an important variable for the ongoing overall health of a partnered relationship.[56]

Lest we miss the real essence of what's important in sex, it is the experience of emotional and spiritual intimacy. The actual physicality just serves as the pleasurable conduit. Our understanding of this is vital to sustaining connection, even as our libidos may decline or other physiological limitations may arise.

In writing this essay, I have successfully resisted the impulse to look up the definition for the word *intimacy*. I have heard over many years in my therapy practice the use of the word *intimate* as a euphemism for sex. I've always found it interesting when couples use this substitution to describe their sex lives, especially when I see and hear of the stuck character in their overall relationship. Ultimately, it is presumptuous of me to question the semantical accuracy of replacing the phrase *being intimate* for sex.

I define intimacy as a deep quality of knowing another person. It requires intention and presence. Of course, this will ebb and flow for any of us. Life is busy and unpredictable at times. I think it is fair to say intimacy allows for an aggregate experience. Intimacy marries intention and presence through the senses. Our physical needs may require adjustment due to age-related factors. There is never a change in the need for intimacy. In other words, the sex may wane, but the intimacy must remain.

There are experiences we each have had through one or more of our five senses that instantly have pulled us out of the to-and-fro of the day and zeroed-out time. Ever bit into a stunning piece of key lime pie or authentic New York cheesecake? Been slowed and lifted simultaneously by hearing a transcendent piece of music like Albinoni's *Adagio in G Minor*? Been warmed inside and out by the smell of wood smoke or of suntan lotion intermingled with salt air? Of course, some of you reading these past few lines have either shrugged your shoulders or possibly scrunched your faces at the thought of these things. What's pleasant for some is not always pleasant for others.

While we cannot be intimate with food or music or smells in the context of our deliberation, these experiences illustrate the trueness of intimacy. Intimacy is inherently individual but paradoxically requires a partner. We each have our own combination of experiences, passions, proclivities, and purposes. These are fine in and of themselves, but to experience intimacy, we need these to be seen by the other.

Another component of intimacy that is absolute is the suspension of judgment. We are wired for and spend the majority of our waking experience in some level of judgment. This is not necessarily a pejorative act. It is simply how our brains are wired. To reach the fullest experience of intimacy, we come to the level of presence that is both interactive and observant while being absent the inward turn to judgment. Judgment both requires and creates distance, and while this is necessary and protective at times, it is also an impediment to intimacy.

This brings us to the final necessary element of intimacy: vulnerability. If we fully suspend our ability to judge, we are exposed. We are no longer in a position to readily step into a protective posture as indicated by our read of the situation at hand. And if we are in a default position of protection, this denies our partner access to a clear view of us, thus blocking them from fully engaging and being intimate with us. The further we stretch into the Third Age, the greater the potential that we may succumb to default protective postures due to past hurts. We'll see one example of this in the next essay—following a poem and original fictional vignette. The work of arriving at intimacy is, at times, cold and viscous. Once there, we can relax for a time, as in a perfectly warm bath complete with the softening oils and smells that envelop us like a mother's womb.

The scene in *The Kominsky Method* isn't really about intimacy, per se. Sandy and Lisa seem to like each other, but it is early in the potential relationship. Lisa is trying to get her bearings after coming out of a long-term marriage, and Sandy is loaded with enough emotional blockages to derail a speeding commuter train. Intimacy, still and always a need, will peer through the recesses and clouded lens from time to time for Sandy. And so his work continues.[57]

★★★

Choices
With untold numbers lying about
Slowly dying in the noontime sun,
A young dancer pirouettes and throws another starfish
Back into the emerald sea.
Love is a choice.

The husky bearded farmer stands,
His family's labor generations deep,
Poached by outsiders and elites.
Now as his siloed stores darkly rot,
He brandishes 100 rounds of black fire.
Fear is a choice.

An unwelcome prophet returns home.
His dark mother now childless,
Her muffled wails rattle the embracing bosom
Of the protesting stranger.
Love is a choice.

With the black comb missing three random tines,
The pale daughter spews bile, finds the faint part
And strums the strands of stray, silver hair

On her dying father's head.
The disease didn't have to happen this way.
Fear is a choice.

The gallant knight presses forward,
Undeterred in his quixotic quest
He tilts at the giant windmill,
As Sancho dutifully follows
Humming The Impossible Dream.
Love is a choice.

★★★

A widow of many seasons went for a walk down the block in her South Chicago neighborhood, normally ill-advised given the dangers of the streets. She needed the sharp, late October evening air to focus her addled mind. She had just received a text from her estranged son, confirming the worst. Her Sweet Pea was back in the hospital. The precious six-year-old's body would not withstand the ravaging invaders this time.

The woman's tears were frosting her creviced cheeks. Against herself, she began humming a favorite spiritual, a song she'd learned when she herself was just six years old. The tune caught in her throat. The church of her youth was just two blocks over. It was now overrun by rival gangs, one to which her son belonged. The church marked the dividing line between their territories, though, this didn't matter much to the widow. She had left this sanctuary many years before.

Suddenly, she heard a grunt coming from a darkened corner of a tenement stoop.

A decrepit, shoeless beggar with a gnarled, gray beard and a fraying, oversized, black wool coat listed toward her. She was used to seeing the neighborhood drunks and addicts from behind her barred windows, but since the new shelter had opened, there was relatively little loitering on this street in the evenings, especially with the weather turning colder. She didn't recognize this man.

"Excuse me, young lady," he said through a dysphagic gurgle. "I know that song you're humming. That's 'Wade in the Water.'" Then he started to mutter the words off key. "Wade in the water. Wade in the water, children. Wade in the water. God's gonna trouble the water."

Something about this man caused the widow to stop and listen.

"If it's not too much trouble, will you sit with me a while and sing?" he asked, holding her steady gaze. "Your voice brings this tired soul peace."

The widow was drawn to him, feeling no sense of danger, nor certainty, just presence.

The pair sat down against the side of the building, and she began to sing, heavy, almost in tenor tones. The stranger's broad shoulders dropped, and he released an easy breath across his scaly, purple lips. She felt his coming death throbbing in her core.

When she finished the song, he looked over to her, penetrating her with his low brown eyes. "You have been kind to this forgotten, dying man. For your kindness, I will grant you three wishes."

The woman laughed. "What? Is this a Brothers Grimm fairy tale? This is Southside Chicago. And do I look like a woodcutter to you?" She laughed again.

He didn't respond, but his eyes penetrated further. This unsettled her.

She cleared her throat and narrowed her eyes. "Look. I'm not religious, but this reminds me of Jesus's time in the desert. The Devil offered him the world, the universe even." She paused. "You're not the Devil, are you?"

The old man smiled. "I'm just sayin', there's more to life than what's right in front of us."

She stared ahead before turning to him. "Okay. For my first wish, I wish that no one ever be granted any more wishes, including me."

It was now the man's turn to fix his stare. "Are you testing me? Do you not believe me? What about your granddaughter? What about the violence and poverty that surrounds you daily? What about your son and his gang activities? Your dead husband?"

The widow drew a sharp breath. "H-how did you..." She swallowed hard. "I-I still stand by my wish." She turned aside and bit her lip. Another tear crossed the outside corner of her lower eyelid and stuttered down her face.

The decrepit beggar smiled. "You have chosen so very wisely, my child. Follow me." He struggled to rise.

More addled now, in spite of herself, she brushed her tears against her coat sleeve, grabbed his elbow and forearm, and helped foist him to his unsteady feet. She maintained her grip as he guided her up the few steps to the apartment door.

He put his hand on the doorknob, paused, and turned to her. "Why did you choose to erase all wishes for all time? Do you feel you don't deserve good things?"

Her tone was now like the late evening cold Chicago air—measured, spare, and quick. "I deserve Life, just like everyone else. And Life is hard … and joyful. It always has been and always will be. Wishes will never be greater than Life."

The beggar shook his head and muttered, "So very wise."

In a singular motion, he opened the door, released the knob, and swept his arm upward, opening a portal, shimmering through a translucent wave, onto a hilltop. The pair could see a menagerie of scenes. Children, still in unremitting pain from their diseases, yet showing no signs of distress. They even mustered faint smiles at the gentle care they were receiving from loved ones. The aggrieved standing nearby, whose children of any age had died, were being embraced by strangers holding vigil. Working-class fathers were singing while attending to their requisite duties of home and hearth. There was great variety in presentation, style, and means, but there was no discernible conflict. Difference nourished the soil; equanimity wafted in the air. Peace pervaded the land.

"What is this?" the widow asked.

"You know what this is," the man chuckled. "This is heaven."

"But I told you I'm not religious. And why is there still pain here?"

"It's so amusing to me that the very one whose wisdom opened the one true door suggests that she does not understand the fruit of her wisdom. No, of course you're not religious. No. But you are a true believer. Look again."

This time, to one side, a vision of her very neighborhood lay. As the scene rotated, she saw herself, first standing arm-in-arm with her son. They were both crying, looking down at the tombstones in the churchyard. Her husband's stone stood vigil next to the fresh burial of her granddaughter's. The next scene was her watching as her son was removing the bars from outside of her living room windows. Nearby, a former rival gang member held a fresh can of paint.

This is my take on the proverbial three wishes story. There are several variations across Northern and Western European folklore. In other traditions, the numbers and symbols may vary, but they all ground in an examination of an individual's, and a community's, values. It feels a bit ironic that protagonists who hold integrity to values of humility and service to others are commonly rewarded in the end with gratuitous material wealth. It's an understandable desire for a people at a time of widespread scarcity to receive a sudden earthly riches windfall. But it feeds, at best, a distorting view of the gritty experiences of life; at worst, it fosters a magical thinking that, sooner or later, has people blindly banging into walls where they expected open doors. This leaves many, far too many, people feeling hurt and isolated and impotently wishing for an end to their pain and loss. I'm not suggesting people should abandon hope. But hope for a material solution is not hope, it is a wish, a desire, and it runs the great risk of having a short half-life.

Dalai Lama's thoughts on the matter:

> I say to people that I'm not an optimist, because that, in a sense, is something that depends on feelings more than the actual reality. We feel optimistic, or we feel pessimistic. Now, hope is different in that it is based not on the ephemerality of feelings but on the firm ground of conviction. I believe with a steadfast faith that there can never be a situation that is utterly, totally hopeless. Hope is deeper and very, very close to unshakable.[58]

Following the sage words of Dalai Lama calls us to carve space for both our conviction of more to come that will offer joy and restoration and the inescapable experiences of pain and loss in our lives. Hope does not exist without both of these.

The Japanese writer Haruki Murakami coined the phrase, "Pain is inevitable. Suffering is optional." Mr. Murakami draws his quote from ancient Buddhist writings, which put forth the equation, "Pain times the non-acceptance of the pain equals suffering." There is much value in the Four Noble Truths at the heart of Buddhism. I briefly referenced these pillars earlier. A fuller distillation of these goes as follows: Life is suffering; Suffering comes from attachments; Non-attachment is the antidote to suffering; Following a path of non-attachment leads to enlightenment.[59]

When I consider these tenets of Buddhism, I recognize both their value and their limitations. It's easy to see the correlation between attachment and suffering. However, if we approach this from a neuroscience lens, our brains are actually hardwired for attachment. Our DNA is encoded for social connectivity in order to thrive. We can do no other. So, what we really need to focus on is over-attachment, that state of being which excludes a life beyond the persons or things that give us buoyancy and definition.

When we consider the connective ground zero that is our most cherished relationships, we quickly arrive at the marrow of these experiences: expectations. And expectations have nothing to do with hope and everything to do with desire. I promise I am not the new spokesperson for the Wet Blanket Society. I am not suggesting we endeavor to erase all desires from our lives. Rather, I am advocating for a regular self-audit, to assess how we are managing the pursuit and enjoyment of our desires in relation to how we are accepting closures and losses in our lives. The less balance we have with this, driven by unrealistic expectations, the greater our struggles, both internally and within the relationships we still have. Healthy expectations are defined but pliable. They help us focus our choices and responses to our time and place. They are mutable as we take in more information and experiences.

I was seeing a couple who had been married for forty years. Larry and Lynn arrived at my office in a state of deep rupture. Larry readily owned that, over the years, his work and hobbies had taken great precedence over his care and cultivation of the marriage—he had retired five years prior to meeting me. He was penitent and eager to do all he could to make amends. For her part, Lynn came in with a newfound sense of self-power and fortitude. She was no longer going to accept his inattentiveness. But, sadly and understandably, she was stuck in the past forty years. She repeatedly took charge in the sessions, dictating terms for not only her husband but also me in my role as therapist. She would then continually change the standards she had set for Larry. Though clearly bitter and lonely, she kept insisting she was happy now and was in her "case of contentment."

Experiencing pain and rejection over many years is a tragedy. Creating a thin veneer of contrived peace is an even greater tragedy. Lynn was unable to attend to her wounds in a healthy way. Refusing to be another statistic in the rising gray divorce phenomena, she chose to move into the couple's second home at the lake and carry forward in her case of contentment. Joylessly, she is encased.

Larry, for his part, is feeling the pain of this loss. He continues to work to accept the new parameters in the marriage, which are wholly composed of minimal and superficial interaction, almost exclusively to occur around larger family events. In accepting this pain and loss, he is slowly able to turn to connections at church and in the community. He has even taken up the craft of brewing beer, saying it requires great patience, attention to detail, and a tolerance for repeated failure, all things he regrets not engaging in more over the length of his marriage to Lynn.

The older we are, the more we lose. This is a simple truth. But, depending on our perspective, there is also the potential for more gains. We can always summit new ground in age and understanding.

I recently played a gig at a small venue at the beach. I noticed an elderly man sitting with whom I presumed to be his wife. I was mixing original songs with beloved covers from the '60s and '70s. He sang along to each one, even scrabbling his way through my originals, which I was fairly certain he had never heard before. After each song, he would raise his arms and clap slowly and demonstrably, with the broadest smile. He came up to me afterward and expressed his appreciation for my music. He then segued into talking about his joy through this time of life, despite some unwelcome changes and losses.

"You know," he said, "soon after I turned sixty-five and retired, my wife died suddenly. After the funeral, everything settled down, and people went back to their lives. 'What the hell do I do now?' was my first and frequent thought." He spoke of beginning to drop into depression, ruminating on passive and diffuse wishes for things to get better. "Then one day, an old Scottish proverb popped into my head. 'If wishes were horses, then beggars would ride.' The next thought came: 'I've never been sixty-five … or sixty-five and widowed before. There's so much to learn.' Now I'm seventy-two. Well, I've never been seventy-two before. There's still so much to learn and do. I wake up each day, excited to see what life will be like in that moment. If it hurts, I know that tomorrow will be a new day and a new experience." He smiled and pointed over in the direction of the lady waiting for him. "My girlfriend can attest to that."

★★★

Cockatiels are usually gentle, affectionate birds. They get so excited upon seeing their humans, greeting them with chirps, songs, and the banging of their favorite toys against their cages. They bond fiercely with their person and can even become jealous and demanding of time and attention. Huh … not so different from most of us, actually. They love cuddling and music. There is a hilarious YouTube video of a man playing his acoustic guitar and singing Elvis's *Don't Be Cruel* to his two cockatiels who are sitting side by side on a perch. One remains stoic while the other bobs, sways, and gyrates in time with the beat. Eventually, the second one goes into full Broadway finale, stretching its wings wide and thrusting its head to the clear annoyance of the first.

Derek, a former client of mine, is a genial man in his late sixties. An introvert who played against type for much of his life, he is easily likeable with his boyish mop of thick, brown hair; quiet, dewy eyes;

and mild, closed-lipped smile. He came for help with acceptance of and living with his recent diagnosis of progressive supranuclear palsy (PSP), a late onset neurodegenerative disease similar to, and often mistaken for, other conditions including Parkinson's and Alzheimer's. This is the same condition Linda Ronstadt has, and like Ms. Ronstadt, it began robbing Derek of his post-career passion: playing music for children.

Following lengthy careers in the military and civil service, Derek began playing guitar and singing self-penned songs for children in settings such as schools, summer camps, and hospitals. Just before retiring three years earlier, he went through an unexpected, and painful, gray divorce. His path to recovery was to thrust himself fully into his new passion. He had been playing to growing audiences across a greater geographic reach until a few months before we met.

In our first session, he spoke of Lucy, his companion, repeatedly referencing his time with her and how helpful she was. When I asked what Lucy had to say about his condition, he stopped and curled one side of his mouth. He realized he hadn't mentioned that Lucy was his pet cockatiel.

One of my favorite pastimes over the past thirty-plus years is spending Saturday mornings listening to NPR's *Weekend Edition Saturday* with Scott Simon. On one particular Saturday in March of 2021, when yet another surge of the COVID-19 pandemic was taking hold, during his opinion segment, Simon acknowledged the indiscriminate toll the virus was exacting on people of all makeups and creeds. He then pivoted to the surprisingly wonderful world of cow-cuddling. He spoke of how, during the pandemic, people were paying to cuddle cows. "The cows are willing to be hugged, even eager." Owing to the impact of the virus, he quoted Suzanne Vullers, owner of Mountain Horse Farm in Naples, New York. "You cannot hug your friends, or hug your grandkids, but you can hug Bella and Bonnie."[60]

The solid science undergirding this therapeutic experience, long practiced in the Netherlands, rests in these large, warm animals having slower heartbeats. The act of embracing them can produce oxytocin, the social bonding hormone—also known as the "love drug"—in humans and other mammals alike.[61]

In addition to the hit of oxytocin, we have the support of mirror neurons at work. Mirror neurons, first discovered by researchers working with macaque monkeys in the early 1990s, are specialized brain cells that fire both when a particular action occurs and also when the noted action is only observed in another.[62] This can help explain how we "read" another person's mind and how connections are fostered and reinforced. The manifold implications of this discovery are guiding important work in empathy across many specific neuropsychological areas today.

Additional evidence is suggesting mirror neurons are not exclusive to primates or even mammals—yes, your beloved dog or cat can read your mind, if they so choose. Researchers have discovered mirror neurons in the brains of songbirds that fire both when the animal is singing, as well as when listening to similar melodies of another songbird.[63]

I wrote the *Goodwill Vulture's Club*, a three-part children's chapter book series several years ago to highlight the generative and healing bonds we experience with certain animals. Extensive research for the series introduced me to delightful examples of both traditional and nontraditional animal connections. Many of us are familiar with the love we have with dogs and cats. More and more, these two species are showing up in hospitals, dentists offices, on college campuses, and even in airports to offer their steadfast, unconditional support to the anxious or bereaved. I've seen several heart-rending videos of advanced dementia patients, often long-term mute, seemingly coming back to life when in the presence of a gentle dog. Nontraditional animals brought into therapeutic roles include llamas in nursing homes and even guinea pigs being used to increase prosocial behaviors in children with autism. The list goes on. Anyone try goat yoga?

Aggressive animals notwithstanding, and allowing there are persons who, for medical limitations or traumatic histories, may not be able to engage with certain animals, our connections with these gentle beings are a lifesaver for so many more. Derek did not grow up with animals due to a severe allergy issue for his brother. Given a similar issue for his ex-wife, over the course of his career and family life, they sought connection through other means, some effective, some not so much. After his divorce, it was his daughter who talked him into meeting Lucy, the twelve-week-old, fuzzy, towheaded, diva alien that would become his new best friend in no time. Derek has a tough path in front of him, but I am confident he will continue to find emotional sustenance and succor with his daughter, his friends, and, yes, his companion Lucy.

Life changes in the instant. The ordinary instant.
–Joan Didion, *The Year of Magical Thinking*

I knew my coworker Marilyn for ten years, the duration of my time working for the county mental health center. Demure, respectable, assiduous in her work as an administrative assistant, she went about her job with a gracious and understated presence. Every time I saw her, she smiled. It was near the end of my ten-year term when Marilyn crossed the thirty-year threshold and decided to retire. On her final day, with her desk having been cleared the day before, she came with her husband Paul to a fitting fete in the main conference room. For many of us, myself included, this was our first time meeting Paul. Like his bride of many years, he carried himself with restraint but also subtle Southern charm. He sat dutifully and happily next to Marilyn, eating cake while she opened presents and notes of well-wishes.

No one expected her to give a speech, but when asked about her retirement plans, Marilyn beamed. "We're gonna love on those grandbabies, but first," she said with a glint in her eye and her right index finger pointing upward, "Paul and I are leaving this weekend for a cruise to the Caribbean."

When I arrived at work the next day, the air was somber and still. The absence of light chatter was conspicuous. I turned the corner to my cubicle section and ran into my normally affable supervisor. She greeted me with a solemn "hi." Before I could ask, she added,

"Marilyn's husband had a massive heart attack and died just after they got home last night."

Stunning news. Displacing and jarring.

Immediately, I thought of a quote from Joan Didion's piercing memoir *The Year of Magical Thinking*: "A single person is missing for you, and the whole world is empty."[64]

Meeting someone, seeing someone under predictable, everyday life circumstances only to hear of their sudden death is challenging for anyone. We all felt a deep sadness for Marilyn, who was understandably devastated. The office pall lasted for a few days before a natural migration coalesced back into the hum and rhythm of our work days.

Over the coming weeks and months, we would get updates from Marilyn's close friend and coworker. Light on details, given Marilyn's private nature, we were glad to hear of her finding her footing with her original plan to spend lots of time with her grandchildren. Moving on from that job myself, I lost touch with Marilyn's path and family. She didn't strike me as one who would venture back out into the world of dating and a new relationship. My wish for her wasn't predicated on that per se. I just hope she found fulfillment and peace.

Joan Didion's book chronicled the first year following her husband's, fellow writer John Dunne's, sudden death. In one particular anecdote, she described seeing his shoes in the closet and having the automatic thought, "He'll be home soon." What was even more remarkable was that her only daughter Quintana fell ill from the flu, which quickly morphed into pneumonia and sepsis. She was placed in a medically induced coma just days before John's death. She nominally recovered months later only to fall and suffer a head injury. Quintana died less than two years after her father, just months before *The Year of Magical Thinking* was published.

Joan Didion wrote, "I know why we try to keep the dead alive: we try to keep them alive in order to keep them with us. I also know that if we are to live ourselves there comes a point at which we must relinquish the dead, let them go, keep them dead."[65]

These are strong words from Ms. Didion. I suspect some would find them strident, while others soothing, a permission of sorts to go forward in life following these relationships that held such power and import in our lives. If we are to have more high-quality living in the years, perhaps decades, ahead after losing a loved one, we have to find a place in our psyches to situate and honor the dead.

Marilyn was able to follow the natural path into an ongoing connection with her remaining family. Joan Didion wrote a subsequent memoir, *Blue Nights*, recounting her experience around Quintana's death and remained engaged with her writing and stage and screen adaptations until her death in 2021. For others, the path following widowhood does wind back into the world of partnered relationships.

Laura Stassi, host of the podcast *Dating While Gray*, had an episode titled "Love After Loss." One of the guests on this particular show was geriatric neuropsychiatrist Peter Lichtenberg. The questions before him included, "What are the differences for someone dating after widowhood versus after divorce?" and "Are widowers looking for an instant replacement?"[66]

Dr. Lichtenberg is in a unique position to answer these questions. His professional experience aligns with his personal story. Dr. Lichtenberg is a veteran of four marriages, widowed twice with one divorce situated in between. He is now happily married to his fourth wife, Debbie. Regarding the difference with dating when divorced versus widowed, he said, "When you're widowed, that relationship is continuing. You're trying to find a place in your life that works for both—the old and new relationship. With divorce, you're trying to let go for good." Regarding dating while still grieving, he specifically added, "You're still vulnerable."[67]

With respect to Dr. Lichtenberg, while I agree more with his premise that you retain some character of the relationship with the deceased spouse, I would contend that vulnerability, in its different forms, is the potential purview of anyone following loss irrespective of that loss resulting from death or divorce.

Despite her call to "relinquish the dead, let them go, keep them dead," I wonder where Ms. Didion traveled in this psychological quest and sincerely hope she found a settled space for John and Quintana in her living world.[68] I suspect Marilyn readily found the place for Paul in the eyes and spirits of her children and grandchildren. Hopefully, for her, this space offered an opening into a future of peace and promise.

★★★

Widowed

"What color is your emotion?" the leader asks.
"What form? Is it two or three dimensional?
Hot or cold?
Coarse or smooth?
Moist or dry?"
He answers with a throat cleared whisper,
"Black, wet, and sticky, like highway tar though cool to
  the touch."
"Ah, yes." The leader nods.
"My old companion. Grief takes on many forms."
She continues to talk,
Words melding into tar, dropping in decibels and coherence.
He rises to leave, parsing and parting the thickened
  particulates.
He will return next Tuesday.
To seek direction,
To seek connection.
47 years anchored,
One year unmoored.

JANUARY 30, 2006

It was late that afternoon when I got the call from my sister Pam saying, "It's time to come."

I wrote in the "Who Are you, Really?" section about the role and experience of care-er, as coined by my friend Frank. My sister Pam has been a nurse for many years, working in varied capacities, from the ER to a cardiology office to patient-and-employee health education. And I am a long-toothed therapist. Among our siblings, she and I have held the traditional caring vocations. Our careers were organic extensions of our experiences growing up as children of divorce with a capricious, alcoholic father and an often-depressed and withdrawn mother. Pam and I, separated by one year and five days, are the middle of four living, full-blood children. In our youth, she and I sleeved relatively naturally into attending to chores at home with Mom. To this day, I still enjoy washing dishes—an act that seems universally complained about. I suppose the act is a touchstone for me, an attempt to ground in a cherished, imperfect time in my life, to be cliché, a simpler time despite the aforementioned challenges in our home. Regular and seasonal chores included dishwashing, gutter-cleaning, grass-mowing, leaf-raking, hanging clothes on the line, and chimney-cleaning. Interestingly, I don't remember much in the way of cleaning my room. To be clear, my mom was the main dishwasher. More often, Pam or I would sweep the kitchen floor after dinner. So perhaps my present-day penchant is a simple act of still connecting with our mom.

Given this history, it's no surprise Pam and I exclusively shared the final two-year journey of caring for our mom. From the initial consult with the oncologist, wherein the three of us heard the words "terminal cancer" and "average life expectancy is two years," we stayed in sync with the rigors and, at times, ease and pause of attending to Mom. I spent many nights of interrupted sleep on hard, unwieldy vinyl hospital recliners punctuated by Mom's guttural distress and confusion. These being the direct results of the tumor invading and spreading within her brain. Pam had her share of restless nights too, including many in her home where Mom spent most of her time when not in the hospital.

My last act of connecting with Mom was the result of Pam's attention to detail in the most sacred of moments. I walked into Mom's room in the care facility to find her unconscious with Pam sitting at her bedside. Our younger sister Beth and a family-friend Orla were standing at the foot of the bed, engaged in a separate conversation. I came and sat beside Mom, opposite Pam. We chatted for a few moments with Pam updating me on Mom's condition. I stroked Mom's coarse gray hair and watched the slow rise and fall of her chest, with interminable separations between each breath. Pam could see my agitation with the distraction of Beth's casual chat at the foot of the bed. She locked eyes with me and asked if I still remembered how to pray the rosary. I nodded. She then pulled out glossy, black beads and handed them to me. The rosary was a gift from Orla's Irish Aunty Ditma, a nun who'd had the beads blessed by Pope John Paul II. Pam then rose and seamlessly asked the other two to join her in the visiting parlor while I prayed with Mom. This was the truest, most fitting final gift for our deeply Catholic mother.

Grief is not linear. Elizabeth Kübler-Ross wrote about the grief stages and qualified the process as uneven, stages skipped and revisited.[69] I would add that grief, in its fullness, is three-dimensional. It is the stories that illustrate and color our lives with the lost loved one. This animation is the enzyme that moves us through the process of integrating our losses and adds to the living composite that is us. And that resultant perspective is what we carry forward into our relationships, activities, and sense of our own—and our loved ones'—mortality.

Following the relatively natural order, in regard to physical death, we experience these losses with increasing volume and velocity as we move further into the Third and, hopefully, Fourth Ages. The word *velocity* sounds dramatic, akin to a roller-coaster ride where we have just crested the long, slow climb before hurtling forward and down, jerking side to side as we roll through the undulating curves. It is possible to feel this way if we consider most of us experience little in the way of physical death in our younger years. Acceptance of impermanance—the one absolute in life—is a hard-earned perspective that can buffer us from this out-of-control sense. The degree to which we resist the acceptance of our losses leaves us stuck in grief, usually in the places of sadness or anger.

The "Black, wet, and sticky" from the previous poem.

There are many quality books written on the subject of grief, offering insights and ideas on how we might go about the work of healing and integrating loss. There are also many wonderful hospice programs that include activities, counseling, and care for the newly bereaved. Among the suggested activities are memorials and rituals. One specific activity involves creating a memory box, a trove that includes particular mementos and keepsakes, valued reminders of our loved ones. These tangible cues and anchors represent stories, often repeated, that are the soft tissue and sinew of our relationships.

Were I to make a memory box about my mom, among many other items, it would include a dried dandelion flower, a small plate, a replica of an ecology flag, a picture of Sarah Vaughn—Mom's favorite velvet-voiced jazz singer—a ticket stub for the musical *Hair*, and a Chicago Cubs baseball.

The summer of 2004 was a high point for Mom. After a grueling course of chemotherapy in the spring, which left her so frail and feeble, she began to regain some strength and vitality. And she was lucid. Being the long-suffering Chicago Cubs baseball fan I am—that suffering was briefly interrupted by their first World Series championship in 2016—I invited Mom to join me on a trip to Chicago to see the Cubs play and to visit with her sister Carol and nephew Allan, who were living two hours west in Freeport, Illinois. That trip is now ensconced in my memory, an oasis in the midst of the most barren of seasons.

Mom still moved slowly and gingerly. I accounted for this by allowing ample time to get from the hotel to Wrigley Field. She wanted to take the Chicago subway—also known as the "L"—to relish the day and soak in some memories of her youth. My mom was born and raised in Milwaukee, Wisconsin. During my youth, she seldom spoke of the time and experiences of her own youth. While not intending our Chicago trip to be a fact-finding mission, I, nonetheless, was pleased to hear some of my mom's memories spoken aloud. An example of this was my unobtrusive, yet resolute, mother sharing tales of how she and her girlfriends would occasionally skip class from West Milwaukee High School and take the bus down to Chicago to see a Cubs game. Standing on the subway platform, I just smiled and said, "I never knew that about you, Mom."

When I shared this story with Pam, she told me Mom and her girlfriends would more often skip school to go see the Milwaukee Braves practice. Milwaukee County Stadium, home of the Braves, was basically in the backyard of West Milwaukee High. Pam then added that Mom should have married a baseball player.

Growing up, I was a natural and gifted distance runner. I was also a good basketball player, but my favorite sport was baseball. And I was mostly terrible at it. I finally threw in the towel on playing baseball when first introduced to curveballs around age twelve. However, my love for the sport remained and rooted on the spectator side. I never knew some seminal strand for this passion resided on the X chromosome bequeathed to me by my mother.

A mild Chicago day culminated with dinner after the game at a German restaurant where we met Carol and Allan. I have a picture—a sneaky way to capture events outside time—of the three of them at the table, my mom flashing the brightest and deepest smile of her last two-year journey. That picture would be added to the items in the memory box to represent those final couple of years.

ANDROCLES AND THE LION

Let me tell you about *Androcles and the Lion,* one of Aesop's fables:

A slave named Androcles once escaped from his master and fled to the forest. As he was wandering about, he came upon a Lion lying down, moaning and groaning. At first, Androcles turned to flee, but finding that the Lion did not pursue him, he turned back and went up to him.

As he came near, the Lion put out his paw, which was all swollen and bleeding, and Androcles found that a huge thorn had got into it and was causing all the pain. He pulled out the thorn and bound up the paw of the Lion, who was soon able to rise and, like a dog, lick the hand of Androcles. Then the Lion took Androcles to his cave and would bring him meat every day from which to live.

But shortly afterward, both Androcles and the Lion were captured, and the slave was sentenced to be thrown to the Lion, after the latter had been kept without food for several days. The Emperor and all his Court came to see the spectacle, and Androcles was led out into the middle of the arena. Soon, the Lion was let loose from his den and rushed, bounding and roaring, toward his victim.

But as soon as he came near Androcles, the Lion recognized his friend and fawned upon him and licked his hands like when they first met. The Emperor, surprised at this, summoned Androcles to him, who told him the whole story. Whereupon the slave was pardoned and freed and the Lion let loose to his native forest.[70]

★★★

Aesop was a Greek fabulist and storyteller noted for his sage accounts of moral living. The story of Androcles and the Lion is held up as the embodiment of gratitude. However, when I first read the story, I indiscriminately considered it to be more about transaction and quid pro quo. Upon further reflection, I now see the spirit of gratitude permeating through the exchanges between the slave and the lion. The choices of both Androcles and the Lion feel deliberate, both conscious and indwelling, drawing from, in a sense, an unbidden source. In other words, "I don't have to, but I want to."

The Odd Couple was among the most beloved television sitcoms of all time. One of the iconic and oft-copied storylines, "You Saved My Life," involved Felix being grabbed by Oscar just as he was falling out of the high-rise apartment window. What follows is Felix's myriad attempts to repay Oscar, which only serve to increasingly annoy Oscar. Oscar then contrives repeated ways for Felix to "save" him, thus, repaying the debt. Alas, each of these attempts results in further fiasco wherein Oscar has to save the day and unwittingly deepen Felix's sense of obligation.[71]

In a variation on this theme, in an episode of my all-time favorite sitcom, *M*A*S*H*, BJ is in a bind and has to borrow two hundred dollars from Winchester. This ignites the tiring pomposity of Winchester lording this debt over BJ.[72]

Both examples are classic storylines highlighting the power of perceived indebtedness. Completely transactional. Completely devoid of a spirit of gratitude.

I have worked with many couples over the years in my counseling practice. Jim and Anne were one such pair who always impressed me with their dedication and devotion to one another. Having been married for thirty-eight years, including raising two boys through the various joys and tribulations of youth, Jim and Anne came to the anticipated time of their lives wherein they would downsize into a nice retirement community and enjoy a balanced life of purpose and leisure. Jim spent the length of his career in finance, assiduously attending to the facts, figures, and forecasts that permeated his daily schedule. In retirement, Jim extended and enhanced his intentional practices of remembering and acknowledging birthdays, anniversaries, and other dates of importance with personal notes, small gifts, and calls to friends and family. Ceding slight ground to eroding recall, Jim is accustomed to filling his calendar with various and sundry notes and reminders to continue this important practice. "It's about honoring these folks," he said once during a counseling session. He also found familiar terra firma in being a member and leader with the community finance committee.

Anne, after burnishing an early and promising career as an attorney, turned to the attendant roles of mother and homemaker. Along the way, she gave her time and talents to school, civic, and community-based causes that held high meaning for her. For Anne, these activities were not cliché placeholders. She is a self-possessed and gracious person who holds firm to her beliefs and values.

Together, Jim and Anne found and worked to sustain their shared rhythm through those many years of marriage.

With Fate being the sometimes-fickle character, soon after Jim's retirement, Anne was diagnosed with colon cancer. She successfully completed the challenging courses of therapy just in time for Jim's diagnosis of Parkinson's disease. These are the experiences that can disorder one's life, not only for the individual in question but also for the loved ones. Or they can reorder one's life. For Jim and Anne, through time and trial and, yes, a global pandemic, they have come through disorder to an evolving quality of reorder.

What has been the catalyst for this transformation? The practice of gratitude.

I love that phrase, *practice of gratitude.* It takes an abstraction, a state of mind, and makes it material. There is a flurry of contemporary research that looks at the intentional practice of gratitude, primarily in the form of journaling, making lists, and writing letters. When maintained as a regular practice, the empirical data shows consistent improvements in one's overall mental health.[73]

I was chatting with Jim and Anne at a particular ebb point. Anne was struggling with her perception of Jim's inertia and passivity in the face of Parkinson's. "He could be doing so much more to stem the advance of this disease. More therapies, more exercises. Yoga. Anything. It feels like he is just resigned to this. It feels selfish to me." While Jim didn't align with all of Anne's thinking, he was quick to acknowledge and validate her experience. He also acknowledged his own moments of despair in contrast to his default penchant for optimism and charity.

In the midst of this stuck point, Anne decided to start journaling about gratitude. When I saw them a few weeks later, the room around them was brighter and lighter. Anne gave voice to this transformation resulting directly from her simple evening practice. "It's helping me to accept what is happening. It's helping me to see Jim's efforts and to be more patient with his struggles." Jim in turn spoke to how much it lifted him to see Anne's greater equanimity. Her happiness is an essential part of his happiness. That's what thirty-eight years of mutual respect, dedication, and love will get you.

A. J. Jacobs is a journalist and self-described human guinea pig. He has written several books detailing his experiments with such things as reading the entire *Encyclopedia Britannica* collection and living for a year in full conformance with the rules laid forth in the Bible. Most recently, he turned his attention to the active experience of full gratitude. The culmination of this is his book *Thanks a Thousand*. This book details his efforts to thank the hundreds of individuals across the world who had a hand in creating the cup of coffee he bought at his nearby coffee shop—from the growers and field hands, to the logo designer, the truck drivers, and even the individual who created the design for the cup lid. Allowing that this was a hyperbolic exercise, one of the intriguing results was the repeated experience of surprise on the part of the recipients at being thanked. It is such an uncommon and indeed, in many instances, an unprecedented experience. Thus, we see the spirit and power of gratitude begin to emanate, not as quid pro quo but rather as an infectious mindset that orients us to the good in ourselves and directs us to seeing it in others around us.[74]

In an interview on the *TED Radio Hour*, Jacobs referenced three individuals with keen insights, direct or indirect, about gratitude: engineer and co-inventor of the iPhone Tony Fadell, novelist Chimamanda Ngozi Adichie, and Benedictine monk David Steindl-Rast. Fadell spoke of the first step to gratitude being that of noticing.[75]

Harkening back to the work of Bruce Lipton cited earlier in this section, habituation is the typical state of our neuro-existence. Our brains like to run on autopilot. While this state helps us accomplish many things throughout the course of our days and lives, it is kryptonite to the experience of gratitude.

As seniors, are we more prone to habituation? Or, depending on the choices and structures in our lives, do we have more space for noticing? Time can slow as we age, but with nature abhorring a vacuum, how do we consciously choose to notice what's around us? How do we notice who's around us?

This brings us to the Nigerian novelist Chimamanda Ngozi Adichie. Her stories speak to the history and tragedies of Nigeria, stories that are further fading amongst the latest generations of the diaspora. She gave a TED talk about the danger of a single story. She spoke of how, too often, the stories of a person, place, or thing are "flattened," resulting in a very narrow view. Combine a flattened narrative with habituation, and you have a solid recipe for indifference at best, ingratitude at worst.[76]

True stories are 3D. They are even further fleshed out when we allow the intertwining of one narrative with the myriad others around us in any given context. Life is rich. Life is complex. Jim's experience of Parkinson's is but one narrative within the Venn diagram that is his life, his life with Anne, his life with his family and friends, and so on. This single Parkinson's story threatens to overly define Jim, to overly define his space, to become too loud. His ability to stay with the awareness that it is but one story among many for him, and Anne's ability to stay with this awareness, hold the highest promise for an experience colored and deepened with gratitude. Single stories fuel quid pro quo. Three-dimensional stories foster the active mindset that is gratitude. Taking action based on gratitude amplifies the experience.

According to David Steindl Rast, gratitude begets happiness, a tenet that is well-supported in the research. It's not the other way around, as most may consider. I was struck by a particular sort of syllogism in his TED talk: "If you are grateful, you are not fearful. If you are not fearful, you are not violent." He then added, "You have a sense of enough, not a sense of scarcity."[77]

In the midst of Jim's ongoing journey with Parkinson's, he continues his work on the community finance committee and sends notes and makes phone calls to friends and loved ones, at times honoring what some would consider pedestrian, if not arcane, anniversaries. He has also started to go to Anne's yoga class following their COVID-19 vaccinations. He and Anne even took the time to introduce me to the "finest babka in New York City." They had to special-order it from the store in New York and got it just in time to enjoy before the beginning of Passover.

The practice and living of gratitude.

PART III
Everyone's Truth

Creativity is just connecting things. When you ask creative people how they did something, they feel a little guilty because they didn't really do it, they just saw something. It seemed obvious to them after a while.
—STEVE JOBS

Creativity is available to each of us throughout our lives. It is natural. It is true. In children, we often see the freest manifestation of creativity. It is innocence unencumbered. It is play. It is imagination for its own sake. In adolescence and early adulthood, we witness the more charged energy that is used for discovery and the act of becoming. This is creativity with Polaris purpose. Generally speaking, in the family and career years, creativity is more aligned with utility and supporting the established forms. We have found our respective ways and are seeking to stay on track. In the Third Age, creativity is about new self-discovery—Who am I now?—following a lengthy term of (hopefully) relative stasis. It is also essential in facilitating the synthesis of our histories, in preparation for the closing years. In the Fourth Age, we have creativity available to us as a guiding path to the completion of our corporal lives.

In researching the substance and contexts of creativity, I stumbled across a reference that cited the antonym of the word *creativity* as being *reality*.[78] At first, I found this laughable, though, I can understand and appreciate the intention. Creativity aligns with imagination. If something is imagined, is it real? Not quibbling over the basic truths of the physical universe, isn't everything real at first imagined, or reimagined? Whether we are considering traditional art forms; storytelling; the placebo effect in medicine; or problem-solving in business, industry, or education; what's true is the essence of the creative process that formed the imagined and realized end.

This is a crucial understanding to the pursuit and engagement of creativity for all of us, no exceptions. It goes beyond the necessity of traditional art forms being catalysts for well-functioning societies. We need all manner of creative expression to integrate and improve our world. David Driskell was a bright light and founding father in the world of African American art. Most sadly, he died in 2020 due to complications from COVID-19. Regarding creativity, he had this to say:

> When the indomitable human spirit rises above the chaos of violence, hunger, and pain and soars to a heightened relief through the making of art, we are classless and raceless so long as we create the spiritual vision. As an artist of African ancestry, I have had to learn to live with racism, sexism, and all of the prejudices. I often find refuge and, indeed, solace in the creative process. In the quiet of my small studio nestled in the majestic pines and white birches in Maine, two worlds merge in my work—one of sight, the other of vision. The beauty of nature and the creative world of the imaginations together express the joyous vision I have as an artist, responding to the spiritual urge within to fulfill my earthly task of making and creating my own beautiful world.[79]

Truth. Yours and mine.

What follows in this section are the stories of several Third-Agers who have engaged the creative process in varied forms, in keeping with who they, and their inherent gifts, are.

★★★

Physics "quarky" fact of the day: a hadron is any member of a class of subatomic particles built from quarks and, thus, reacts through the agency of the strong force. With the exception of protons and neutrons that are bound in atomic nuclei, all hadrons have short lives and are produced in the high-energy collisions of subatomic particles.[80]

Um … what?

For many of us, physics is a relatively inaccessible science that serves and informs all life around us but is just beyond the periphery of our senses. When we think of physicists, we conjure images of people in white lab coats, or at least in out-of-fashion, wrinkly, short-sleeved plaid shirts, with tousled hair and, of course, the requisite glasses. It's possible Neil Degrasse Tyson is leading the avant-garde to make over this staid caricature with his animated style and quick smile.

When I watch and listen to Dr. Tyson, it is easy to be impressed by his scientific brilliance. But what impresses me more is his creative mind. The manner in which he takes arcane minutiae and transforms them into accessible and, dare I say, fun information. The truth right before our eyes is physics is the alchemy of science and art. And the source, the Big Bang, of physics is creativity. Each of the most-noted physicists were, and are, blazingly creative: Marie Curie, Albert Einstein, and Katherine Johnson, to name but a few.

I have a friend named David who is a physicist. We met several years ago in a community writers' group. He retired once before heeding the call back to Stanford to work on a project with a few Nobel Prize for Physics winners. Hard to say no to a gig like that. The project was linked with the Large Hadron Collider (LHC). The LHC is, as of the writing of this book, the most powerful particle accelerator ever made. It sits in an underground tunnel at CERN, the European Organization for Nuclear Research, on the border of France and Switzerland. The LHC's function is to push protons or ions to near the speed of light. It consists of a twenty-seven-kilometer ring of superconducting magnets with a number of accelerating structures that boost the energy of the particles along the way.

After this second vocational run, David repositioned to a life of writing excellent crime novels and spending quality time with his wife Sarah and their dog Felicity. When I told him of my interest in writing a book on the themes and experiences of folks in the later part of life, he, with some reticence, agreed to sit down and share a few of his experiences with me. Being a private person, he confessed to some anxiety around the bearing of his story. Assuring him I was not interested in any sort of exposé, I shifted to asking David what he thought creativity to be. He paused, scratched his head, and said, "Well, I'm not very right-brained, but I would say it's taking something from your imagination and making it a reality."

Allowing for the obvious—that David is an accomplished writer—in defaulting to the "right brain" source, he was thinking in the more traditional frame for delineating what creativity is. When I dug deeper with David, he went into talking about his involvement with the recent Stanford project that actually included four Nobel Prize winners and around six hundred physicists in ten countries. I told David this felt like creative rocket fuel to a factor of eleven.

On numerous occasions, I have declared to family, friends, and a few clients that, one day, I would write a book on psychosocial physics. Much of my thinking about the psychosocial experiences of myself and those around me comports nicely with various laws and theories of physics: inertia, entropy, and the observer effect, to name a few. Inertia—an object at rest tends to stay at rest, and an object in motion stays at that same rate or line unless acted upon by some external force—reminds me of the thought and subsequent behavior patterns that characterize our autopilot experiences.[81] When we are feeling good, we happily call this "flow" and sit back and enjoy the ride. When things are lousy, we call this "being stuck or rutted" and sit, haplessly bemoaning our plight, or anesthetize ourselves through one of many vice choices.

Fortunately—or unfortunately, as the case may be—there is also the law of entropy, which is when the amount of disorder from the current system increases and tends toward a state of randomness.[82] Lovely thought, eh? This often occurs naturally at a snail's-on-Quaaludes pace. So, if we had the capacity and time to hang out on a cosmological scale, things would eventually change, for the better or worse.

Luckily for us, we have another component of the law of entropy—you cannot go from a disordered system to an ordered system without inputting energy—plus the observer effect—you cannot attempt to measure or examine a thing, or experience, without changing it. Here is the opening we've all been waiting for: if we don't like something, we can change it. At any, even advanced, age. I mean no disrespect to any of us who may have experienced devastating trauma and loss. We cannot change the material facts of those experiences, but we can work to change our thoughts about the experiences, even if the task is monumental. At the root of this change process is the lens of creativity. We need not blithely or helplessly sit by while entropy works its oft unwelcomed craft. Creativity is about problem-solving and making novel products. We can be active in creating our own transfer of psychological energy in the direction of health and prosperity.

A significant challenge is that creativity, like physics, feels inaccessible to many of us. We live and walk among the select few, those who are genetically endowed with the effortless gifts of manifesting visual and aural works of stunning beauty, such as the word artists who weave lyrical threads, the dancers whose motions move us to tears, and so on. We relegate to the traditional artists the creativity that is inherent to each of us. Creativity is core, like stable protons. Bound to a metaphysical nucleus. Many who achieve fame by living the creative life, especially early on, act more like mesons in the realm of physics, short-lived. I have no understanding of what *mesons* are, but the internet tells me that a meson includes a quark and an antiquark.[83] From these labels, I'll conclude, accurately or not, that they are opposing forces, thus, setting up the strident interaction and subsequent short life. These experiences are not the exclusive purview of the famous. Many of us access, then blunt, our creative source time and again. We have moments wherein the creative energy bursts forth, only to recede into the familiar layering of the mundane. And the familiar has the propensity to dull us.

Bruce Lipton, the developmental biologist introduced in the "Tendrils" section, is noted for his work with epigenetics. In *The Biology of Belief: Unleashing the Power of Consciousness, Matter and Miracles*, he does a remarkable job of linking cutting-edge neurobiological research to the conclusion that we are on the previously referenced autopilot—*subconscious programming* is his phrase—95 percent of the time. He talks about the brain having two parts. First, there's the original brain, the subconscious, which is able to process forty million bits of data from the environment every second. This dominant part of the brain is pattern-seeking, habitual, and can only play back what it learns. Then, there is the cerebral cortex, notably the prefrontal cortex, the area of the brain that facilitates executive functioning, consciousness. This area can only process about forty bits of data per second. Of this, Lipton says, "Self, or consciousness, is an add-on option, and most people don't exercise this option."[84]

With respect to Dr. Lipton's summary frame of the brain's activity, a deeper dive into the inner workings of the brain at any moment shows hundreds of trillions of synaptic interactions occurring within and across these differing regions. We come in and out of greater focus and consciousness like an accordion. In time and context, any of us may be playing an adagio, slow and deliberative, to be cued and followed by a spritely scherzo. It is my intuitive sense that creativity is the musical gestalt, both composer and conductor, arising from the combining of these states of habit and focus.

In other words, creativity is far from just a conscious process. We do need the intention, the focus that is the hallmark of our high consciousness. This is necessary to receive, cultivate, and refine what may come from the unconscious. Within our psyche, we are standing on our mind's curb, watching the flow of taxis along the six-lane road in front of us; each cab represents a thought, many mundane, some destructive, a select few, creative. Answers to issues that are currently vexing us or, at least, the opening direction to resolution. Some cabs don't represent a response to a problem but rather are an expression, an extension of who we are, ready to be released into the world to add to the aesthetic, to facilitate greater resonance and connection. The role of consciousness is to see and hail the right taxi as it approaches.

Creativity happens when we are absentmindedly making our breakfast each morning. It happens when we are in the shower, when we are walking the dog, when we are dreaming. To wit: In the midst of working on this essay, I woke from a dream one night.

As a backdrop to this dream, I have been noticing, with mounting frustration, my declining motor coordination over the past few years. This, along with increasing memory lapses, is motivating me to be more intentional about doing brain exercises to disrupt and even reverse some of this cognitive atrophy. The more conventional, empirically vetted approaches include any number of mindfulness practices, improved diet, sufficient rest, and cardiovascular exercise. All good and true ways to support brain health but also all very common, thus, setting up the risk of being like wallpaper, noticed at first but quickly receding into the passive background and giving way to the stasis of previously autopiloted patterns. I felt I needed something unique, something psychically louder.

Enter the dream: It was a very simple dream actually. A young girl was with her father, waiting to see a teen idol emerge from the back entrance after a concert. When the idol came out, he walked directly by the right-handed girl, smiled, and touched her on the right shoulder as he passed by. She turned, joyfully sobbing, and asked her dad, "Can I be left-handed? I don't ever want to use my right arm again." She wanted to preserve her anointed right arm in popstar perpetuity.

I awoke, recognizing two things: 1) I have another answer to my advancing age concern. In addition to the conventional approaches, I will start prominently using my left hand in as many perfunctory activities as I can. And 2) I have an illustration for the interplay between the conscious and unconscious to use in my book!

You can teach an old dog new tricks, and this old dog wants to learn.
—Thomas P. O'Neill

"Where did I leave those damn car keys? Did I remember to take my pill this morning? What is the name of the lady at church who helps with the food drive? I've only known her for twenty years!"

I've long chafed at the phrase *senior moment*. I suppose it could be the agitation of having a few too many of those occasions myself and not wanting to be reminded of my memory loss feeding my out-of-control feelings. Perhaps. Although, I believe I just prefer not to resign myself to this designation. Yes, it's true my current recall is not up to historical standards. But am I helpless in the face of this evolving, or devolving, experience?

Fran and Gary, both in their early seventies, married two years ago. Fran's first husband died suddenly three years earlier, and Gary had been divorced for fifteen years. They connected through a network of Australian shepherd trainers. I met them through a mutual friend, and together, we had the pleasure of several chats about the wonderful world of dogs. In spite of hearing each reference the pain and hardship of their pasts, there was an ease and malleability that dominated their spirits. Fran's big smile, ruddy cheeks, and short platinum hair fit hand-in-glove with Gary's more straight and milky expression. In one of our conversations, I put the proverbial canine question to them about old dogs learning new tricks. We were having a broader back-and-forth about senior moments that had started with Fran playfully fussing with Gary about not taking his cholesterol medication. Gary copped to a "senior moment" excuse, to which Fran scolded, "That's what those weekly pillboxes with the giant weekday letters are for, you old fart!" Gary grinned and then mumbled about it just not being a habit for him yet. My old dog question was a brief, light insertion, a playful diversion that quickly circled back around to the spotlight on Gary. Fran had him in her loving crosshairs. She pointed a seasoned, calloused index finger at him. "I'd better see you take that pill when we finish here."

Tip O'Neill, the long-time Speaker of the United States House of Representatives, took it upon himself to disabuse us of the particular aphorism, "You can't teach an old dog new tricks."[85] While this is just an old-folk adage, it can feel and look true for many of us or our loved ones as we move into our later years. To add some empirical heft to Mr. O'Neill's pronouncement, many conventional scientific "truths" have wound up on the trash heap of time when revisited via the latest research protocols and superior examination instruments. Ever hear about how our brains are growing from the time in utero up until our mid-twenties, before we crest the summit and then head back downhill from there? Or how all that alcohol you consumed in your younger years killed brain cells you'll never get back? These were the prevailing scientific understandings for a good century or more. Thankfully, in the past several decades, we have discovered neuroplasticity and neurogenesis and have largely turned this older, faulty paradigm on its ear. I was first introduced to these neurological phenomena through the thought-stirring and hope-burgeoning book *The Brain That Changes Itself* by Canadian psychiatrist Norman Doidge. The gist of the book: our brains have fascinating capacities to adapt and regenerate.[86]

It is true we all experience some cognitive decline over time. Anything within the clinical cluster of dementias notwithstanding, we can all relate to "senior moments" when we drop names or forget where we put our reading glasses that are usually sitting atop our heads. Equal, if not greater, is the emotional calcification that can form over time. Alvin Straight's story in the "Tendrils" section is an example of this. We surely get rutted in life.

So ... what of this idea of old dogs learning new tricks? Can they?

Let's go back to this query I put before Fran and Gary. Their answer was not surprising in the least. These dog-training experts described how it is often easier for senior dogs to learn new things as compared to pups. "They have the ability to focus for longer periods of time, and most can more readily adapt to new routines," Fran said, looking pointedly at Gary.

Gary, who was well-set in his ways after being on his own for so long, didn't miss a beat in describing a key variable here being the difference between "can" and "want to." He and Fran had many things to negotiate and work through to learn about each other. They both expressed a gratitude for mutual understanding and patience for each other's slips and foibles, as well as an appreciation for both being willing to try new things and forge new traditions together.

Moving further into the Third Age, how we repeatedly engage our newfound sense of self goes a long way toward helping us explore new interests and activities. It's okay, even good, to "lean on old familiar ways," according to my friend, the songwriter Paul Simon, in his song "Still Crazy After All These Years." We need comfort. We need routine. But we will do well by ourselves to remember it's also okay, even better, to stretch at times, to take advantage of our hard earned mental, emotional, and spiritual capital to keep growing in the direction of healthy living. Our brains are ready and waiting for the opportunity, at every age.

One fascinating footnote to this: there are research accounts of neurogenesis, the forming of new neural cells, occurring even in the immediate aftermath of clinical death. We never stop, never lose, our capacity to learn and grow.[87]

★★★

The Hunt

Cool darkness greets Audrey and me
On this mid-October night.
We are on a hunt.
Her brindled beagle waddle, singular and staccato,
She seeks not perfection, but rather what is right
To release what binds her.
Pungent scents set the pace
And occasionally call for resistance.
My stride is more pressed, angular.
I grow impatient with her process
As I hold to what binds me.
I want to get to the space between the light, where
With the waxing of the crescent moon,
I will claim the vastness of the Orionids.
Audrey hunts the vastness of the earthworm,
Baked and curled on the pavement,
A neglected stone altar offering to the extraordinary not
  missed by her.
In the time it takes a particle of light
To cross a single molecule of hydrogen,
She smells the universe in the dry, lifeless worm.

★★★

The Ma'dan, also known as the "Marsh Arabs," are a semi-nomadic people inhabiting the marshlands of Southern Iraq for over six thousand years. Their cultural and practical ways of living have changed very little over the past few thousand years. The region is prone to severe annual flooding, so the people have adapted to living on floating islands made, structure and supporting platform, of qasab. Qasab is a collective term for a variety of tall, stiff, and reedy plants that grow together near water. The qasab in the areas where the Tigris and Euphrates rivers meet, home to the Marsh Arabs, looks like bamboo and can grow to twenty-five feet tall. In addition to being the building material for the islands and houses, it is also food for the water buffalo and flour for the humans. Talk about sustainability and adaptation in the face of harsh and changing conditions!

The Ma'dan follow a traditional Arab code of honor by which they welcome all guests as equals and do nothing to encourage the guests to leave. They would never say "no" to a stranger in need. This became problematic in the late 20th century when Sadaam Hussein was in power. The Ma'dan were persecuted for being suspected of sheltering dissidents. This culminated in Hussein ordering the draining of the wetlands and the damming of surrounding tributaries. Food became scarce, forcing the Ma'dan out of their homes and off the land. Over time, the Ma'dan dispersed into numerous cities, moving farther away from both their lands and native culture. Only 1,600 out of over a half million Ma'dan were still living in the traditional housing at the turn of the 21st century. Following the fall of Hussein's regime in 2003, coinciding with the end of a four-year drought, the dikes were broken, bringing back roughly half of the former wetlands. The restoration continues to this day.[88]

Closer to home in the United States, we are seeing an uptick of elder, nomadic workampers, a growing group of seniors who were showcased in *Nomadland*, an unorthodox, multiple award-winning film at the 2021 Academy Awards.[89] The movie tells a hybridized account of the life of transient van- and RV-dwellers in the western United States. Fern and Dave, played by Frances McDormand and David Strathairn, are fictional characters interacting with actual veterans of the nomad life. Fern, after a series of unexpected losses, sets out to live the life of a nomad, traveling across many states, living in her converted van, and cobbling together jobs along the way. She meets Dave, and they evolve an uneven connection, which ultimately plateaus as he reintegrates into more traditional society.[90]

I want to take care to not romanticize what would be a very significant and challenging transition, even as it offers great potential. In the case of Fern, the process was somewhat foisted upon her when her husband died. The landslide continued when the entire town in which she lived was scuttled. Her job, her home, and her community

... all gone in a flash. Regrettably, her story is too easily drawn from real life examples. To an appreciable extent, the movie is a social commentary of women and their plights, along with the exploitation of older persons.

The film is unflinching in its portrayal of the hardness of this life, even as we see the joy and unburdening for many of the open-road compatriots. An unidentified woman says, "I love this lifestyle. It is a lifestyle of freedom, and beauty, and connection to the earth. Yet there is a trade-off. You got to learn to take care of your own shit."[91]

Fern learned how to take care of her own shit, figuratively and literally. This included connecting into a resourceful community with Bob Wells, Linda May, Swanke, and the others. Plugging or patching tires, tending to ceaseless engine and other van repairs, gluing back broken dishes, and cleaning out buckets that double as both latrine and table base. These became the understood and accepted financial, physical, and emotional tariffs for the peace of nature and the life of freedom on the road.[92]

Tens of thousands of older Americans are now migrant laborers or seasonal workampers, with the numbers growing every year. In a PBS NewsHour interview, Jessica Bruder, author of the book *Nomadland: Surviving America in the Twenty-First Century*, upon which the movie is based, described the experience of these older Americans:

> These people got caught between flat wages and rising rents, in the failures of retirement finances, in the collapse of the Great Recession.
>
> These are people who realize that, for most Americans, our biggest cost is housing [...] with so much ageism in the workplace [...] a lot of people I met were using this lifestyle as a hack to get around the economic impossibilities that a lot of Americans are facing today. And that made them incredibly creative and resilient.[93]

Cheryl, age seventy-eight, is a widow living by herself in a small, remote log home outside Asheville, North Carolina. I had the good fortune to meet her last year after hearing her son Matt's many accounts of marvel, respect, and angst at his mother's legendary "problem-solving" skills and feats. From unclogging a sink with a plunger to aerating her yard with an old pair of sneakers, roofing nails, and duct tape, Cheryl, it seems, has met no household challenge that has left her daunted. Despite my expectation that she would have a commanding presence given her highly resourceful reputation, she was actually quite soft and unassuming. When I asked her about her sterling domestic engineering CV, she replied a wry smile, "I just sit with things for a while. I'm in no hurry. Something usually comes to me. Younger folks seem to be forever rushing here and there. Of course, they can always consult the Oracle of Google ... or Alexa."

Cheryl's husband died suddenly some twenty years earlier. And just for the record, Cheryl did not develop new practical skills for surviving and flourishing in the aftermath of this unexpected event. As Matt told it, she'd always had this knack, this penchant for keenly observing, musing, and then engaging in addressing said issue with aplomb and inventiveness. This was, however, particularly helpful in the years ensuing her husband's death. Following a work layoff, there were unexpected financial straits for herself and her two teenage boys. She persevered by tightening purse strings, tapping into community resources, and working two jobs.

After both sons finished college, she moved to the mountains of North Carolina near Asheville and began bookkeeping and helping with general chores around a working farm and bed and breakfast. The farm was replete with a modest tract of corn and soybeans, various livestock, and more than one dozen Great Pyrenees dogs—all things she had no prior experience with. In her spare time, she took up arranging and pressing dried flowers. To this day, she continues to be a deliberate and agile learner.

When you think of the word *creativity*, what comes to mind? Caricatures such as pensive, beret-wearing visual or performance artists at the local coffee haunt often dot our mental landscapes. Would you immediately think of practical problem-solving and making novel products or outcomes? Perhaps. I certainly would hope so. Ultimately, the creative process is a challenge of using innate skills to manipulate tools and resources for the expression of an idea or vision. Even this definition, a dry rendering of what many of us consider to be a moist, expressive enterprise, illustrates that the collective creative experience is more expansive than we may think.

As noted in the introduction, the arts and artists are vital to any society. I want us to broaden our perspective of what the creative process is all about so we will see ourselves within its borders. We are all inherent creators. We create every day. We need to produce, not merely for recognition, although that can matter. We need to make products we can put our hands on, be it a piece of art or the shoulder of another whose spirit we touch with our creative brush of kindness and empathy. To be more in touch, more in tune with this, is to direct our "art" in healthy, generative ways.

Specific to the Third Age, where do we fit in this shifting landscape and model of creativity?

There is exciting research that extends beyond the practical benefits of being able to solve problems. When creativity has a focus and a home in our day-to-day lives, the added value for seniors includes greater mental clarity, improved emotional health, and even physical healing, among others.[94]

Want to have a more robust immune system? Aside from an established routine of good sleep, healthy diet, and regular cardiovascular exercise, learn to play and write music.

Want to better manage chronic pain? Volunteer to work with special-needs children, or read novels to the visually impaired.

Want to have better word and object recall? Take up cooking or landscaping with an eye toward exploring new and different ideas.

Want to have a deeper understanding of yourself at this time so you can more easily find and pursue a purposeful life? Do any of these or countless more creative alternatives. And I do mean *countless*. We are all creatives, and therefore, by definition, our options are limitless.

The story of the Ma'dan, though significantly altered by the events of the past thirty-plus years, is not finished. From a people whose very existence was palpably centered on the ability to adapt to a harsh environment, comes simply the latest expression of a harsh environment, albeit a man-made one. The story of the workampers is still being written. Cheryl's story. Your stories and mine. The next chapter in our lives is still being formed. My fervent wish is we all find the creative indwelling to guide and serve us along the way.

★★★

Spiral Staircase

Do what you must,
But do you know what you must?
The sloth was slandered in the common naming department.
His path is patience personified.
He takes hours to climb down from the canopy,
Evading the harpy eagle with pace and color,
To reach his estrus mate.
Ants can move rubber tree plants,
Hauling food twenty times their weight
Back to their waiting queen
Attending to her egg laying task.
Perseverance and resilience see a spiral staircase
And with Lao Tzu, a single step.
Depression sees a circle,
Wearing, droning, and sinking with each rotation.
Death is a flat line, or
The irrational number pi.
After all of the mathematicians have gone home,
The sloth, the ants, you and I,
Will still be here.

A Hare was making fun of the Tortoise one day for being so slow.
"Do you ever get anywhere?" he asked with a mocking laugh.
"Yes," replied the Tortoise, "and I'll get there sooner than you think.
I'll run you a race and prove it."
—FROM *THE TORTOISE AND THE HARE*, AESOP'S FABLES

When life gets you down, you know what you gotta do?
Just keep swimming.
—DORY, FROM *FINDING NEMO*

My friend Dale plopped down in my office. Her thick, graying dreadlocks were typically the only clue to her sixty-three years and newly retired status. Normally, she had a quick smile accenting her alluring amber skin, but for this day, her pressed lips told the fullness of her years and then some. "Hugh, I thought bad things were supposed to come in threes." She swept her middle, ring, and pinky fingers through the air like a conductor. "The refrigerator I just had serviced conked out again. The LED display panel on the microwave went out. How does that even happen? That's two. And then the motor died on my HVAC the other night. That's three, right?" I nodded, and she continued. "Things get old and break down. I get it. Believe me, I do. But I should be good for a while, at least. Right?" Because of her robust good humor and the two of us being longtime Chicago Cubs fans, I was able to tell her that superstitions were only true in baseball, with the exception of the curse of the Cubs billy goat. "Well, you're right about that," she laughed. "Because then I get a phone call this morning, saying my COBRA insurance is balking at paying for my knee replacement. C'mon! I'm getting old and breaking down too."

I then told her this story from my past:

Newly married at age twenty-three, my wife and I spent our honeymoon in St. Thomas. I had been enjoying snorkeling in the translucent waters flowing over the magazine-cover-worthy white sands of the ocean floor, dotted with brightly colored tropical fish and warmly mottled coral. Being young and overly ambitious, I decided it would be fun to snorkel across the bay. I reasoned I was in good shape, and there were no motor boats or ships allowed in this particular harbor, so it would be safe.

And so off I went with my face mask, snorkel, and flippers. I would swim for a time while exploring the underwater wonders and then occasionally look up to get my bearings. About thirty minutes into the swim, I looked up and saw I was about halfway across. I went back to my face-down, real-time Caribbean slideshow and swam for a more extended period of time, transfixed by the beauty below.

I recognized I was getting tired, and my (faulty) internal navigation system told me I should be about three-fourths of the way across the bay. Imagine my surprise when I looked up and saw I was roughly in the same spot I was the last time I had looked up to get my bearings. I had managed to swim a very large circle in the middle of the bay.

Being a veteran of self-imposed precarious situations, I didn't panic but rather shifted my focus. The slideshow was over. The task at hand was terra firma. I began a new pattern of swimming ten strokes and looking up, ten strokes and looking up. This new bi-focal arrangement served me well and deposited me, quite exhausted, on the far shore about thirty minutes later.

When I finished telling Dale the story, and before I could further comment on the importance of shortening one's focus while still keeping an occasional eye on the big picture, she smiled and sang, "Just keep swimming." She reminded me of this song sung by the inimitable Dory the blue tang—the song and character being from *Finding Nemo*, one of Dale's favorite movies to watch with her grandchildren. Dory was on an important journey herself.[95]

Once more, like one of Fran and Gary's Australian shepherds tending to a flock, we find ourselves circling around the meaning and weight of words. What comes to mind when you think, hear, or say the word *old*? If I free-associate on this, I would say, "Declining, not as effective or useful, diminished, frail, limited, slow." Should I stop now? To be fair, in considering the word with regards to people, I would also say, "Familiar, seasoned, and wise." That better? But I'm guessing most of us would rattle off more negative than positive terms. Our modern society does us no favors with much of the marketing and messaging reinforcing the vitality of youth at the expense of the fragility and depletion that is emphasized as a function of greater age. Focusing on the wisdom aspect of many years feels more discrete and targeted, to be used in a limited scope when the need arises. The word *old* is the unquestioned adjective that marks the annual passage of time: one year *old*, five years *old*, forty years *old*, ninety years *old*. The younger we are, we may tend toward, or yearn for, the more positive associations of the word *old* … to a point. The law of diminishing returns eventually gets invoked, and then we use or hear phrases like, "It's all downhill from here."

How do you use the term *old*? How do you think of yourself in terms of your age? I occasionally hear a Third-Ager mark their years with the word *young*. As in, "I'm seventy years young today." I like this attitude and spirit. But it may be a tough sell for those of us with constant reminders of our limitations, be they faltering knees, a less-steady balance, or memory lapses. I like the term *length*. "I'm sixty years long." I know it sounds a bit clunky at first, but try it out. We can't ignore the impact of age on our joints and organs, but let's not lose the hard-earned, and new, benefits of our long years. Other helpful words and concepts that partner well with length are *perseverance* and *resilience.* Staying steadfast in the face of time and trial is doable if we approach it with the right perspective.

Elizabeth "Libba" Cotten was a national treasure. Born in 1893, this self-taught, left-handed, blues-and-folk guitarist, singer, and songwriter was playing and writing songs by age eight. When she was nine, she was forced to quit school and go to work as a domestic. She earned one dollar each month, money her mother saved to eventually buy Libba her first guitar. By her early teens, she wrote her most famous and iconic song "Freight Train."

Given her musical precociousness, it would seem inevitable this would be her path and purpose in life. And it was. But not for another forty years or so. Libba married at age seventeen and gave birth to a daughter named Lillie. Libba then put the guitar down to focus her time and attention on family and church. After Lillie was grown and married herself, Libba divorced her husband and eventually went to work in a department store.

Sometimes, fate is a beautiful thing. Libba had been working just a short time when she found a young child wandering the aisles. She helped the little girl Peggy find her mother who, in turn, asked Libba to come work for them as a maid and nanny to the children. These children included Peggy and Mike Seeger, who would eventually become musical stalwarts themselves, along with their older half-brother Pete. Yes, fate can be a beautiful thing, but it seems to most often require being present, staying steadfast, and persevering.

And so it was in her mid-sixties when Libba picked up her left-handed guitar and set about the fulfillment of her lifelong passion and calling. The great human story is awash with wonderful examples of folks who stayed on their path, allowing for latency and, at times, in spite of obstruction. Within our lifetimes, Grandma Moses, Pauli Murray, and Jimmy Carter are but a few examples of inspiring people finding, fulfilling, or remaking themselves in later years.[96]

After all, the Cubs did eventually win the World Series after a few (okay, 108) years. That's another way to think about length—not one I care for. I spoke with Dale a few weeks after the venting session.

She was happy and relieved to report that, of course, the issues with the appliances were all satisfactorily resolved with some manageable pain to her purse. The greater problem with the insurance coverage was also fixed after dogged perseverance over the phone and online. She had the surgery and then approached the recovery and physical therapy with the same stick-to-it-iveness of one of her favorite singers: Libba Cotten.

★★★

Common Sparrow
I've been told I think too much.
Perhaps.
I suppose when I'm carrying the weight
Of others' expectations,
When I'm wearing the glutinous dread over the looming loss
Of my beloved.
But what of the Earth's inner core,
Or the mantle of ancient ocean floors,
Their colliding plates producing the grandeur
That is the Great Smoky Mountains,
I now stand upon?
If I'm not spending hours each day
Imagining the common sparrow's song,
Coloring these mountain winds
In and through the blue spruce,
Well then,
I'm not thinking enough.

★★★

Growing up in North Carolina, I had the great privilege to spend a week at the beach every summer. A typical day would start in the arcade where I would go through a stack of dimes, playing my favorite baseball pinball game before going out in the midday sun to spend hours in the water. There was an interesting tide that would pull swimmers parallel to the shore rather than out to sea. I would play in the water and, every thirty minutes or so, come out from the sea. Then like a vintage Smith Corona typewriter, I'd walk back up to the original point of entry to go back in.

When walking back, I would invariably do a cursory scan of the beach in front of me, searching for the illusive, perfect conch shell, starfish, or sand dollar. Most of the time, the initial excitement of spying a conch shell rib jutting from the sand would be followed by the disappointment of digging up said conch shell only to find it was badly broken. The rare experience of finding an intact shell was a moment of jubilation, a simple lift for the rest of the trip that even carried over to the return trip home.

In stark contrast to these childhood memories, I took a trip to Cumberland Island, just off the coast of Georgia, in my early thirties. Much of this island is national park land, with limited visitors each year. One morning, I walked out to the beach on the far side of the island and was instantly stopped in my tracks. The beach was littered with perfect conch shells in multitude hues, shapes, and sizes. In my slight stupor, I began picking up shells, marveling at them close up. I hurried back to the inn to get a bag to collect several to take home.

When I stepped back out onto the beach, I had already sidled into what psychologist Barry Schwartz calls the "paradox of choice." Basically, this is a phenomenon wherein too much choice, too much of a good thing, can lead to less happiness and satisfaction.[97] There I was, surrounded by an abundance of pristine beauty, and I began to find fault. I would pick up a perfect conch shell, rotate it in my hand, wrinkle my nose, and toss it back onto the sand. The color wasn't quite what I wanted. The symmetry wasn't just so.

I have previously referenced Sympara, the senior writing group I enjoyed with my friends Tuck and Barbara. Our prompt during one particular session was, "What is surprising to you at this time in your life?" My initial reaction to this question was ... well, a complete void. This was slightly disturbing to me, for if it is true that nothing surprises me, then I'm in deep trouble. To not experience surprise would suggest I am woefully detached from my feelings or maybe walking around with serious scales on my eyes.

Sitting with this question for a while allowed me some time for perspective. I was viewing surprise through the lens of grandeur, the extraordinary events and vistas which seize our breath and shear us into the space outside time. I'm aware this qualifier allows for both joyous and tragic circumstances. Upon further reflection, I was able to refocus my lens and touch surprise in the ordinary. These are the small events that happen perhaps daily—the unexpected phone call from one of my busy daughters; the insight that comes, seemingly from outside me as a gift, helping me to view a problem from a more actionable position; the melody for a new song to write; the chorus of wildflowers along the interstate on a long monotonous drive. Given I have severely curtailed my news intake these days, I was surprised today to have my eyes pulled skyward on my early-morning walk with my beagle Audrey. There, fixed singularly in the dawn firmament was Venus, or perhaps Sirius. It doesn't really matter. While Audrey was busy, nose in the bushes, surveying her own surprise, the star caught me by surprise and gave me joy. It appears these perfunctory events skew strongly toward the positive, the uplifting.

In sum, I suppose what surprises me is I am moving into greater awareness and accessibility of these small surprises. They certainly have been available to me throughout my life, but it is now in my nascent, Third-Age time when they are finding me, and I am finding them.

Surprise in the ordinary, a seeming contradiction, is a beautiful thing.

★★★

Nosey (A Senior Synesthete's Knowing)
While ears and noses don't actually grow
As we continue to age,
They appear so because of gravity and skin changes.
They are listening and tracking
Over misshapen lobes and folds,
Ever available even to the centenarian
Whose nose knows so much.
If curiosity killed the cat,
It was a crime of passion

Or a lover's suicide in pursuit of the unknown.
Unlike Romeo and Juliet,
The cat in me has eight more turns, or
At least two or three,
To see through the eyes of my child,
A toddler's tongue tasting
Sugar and strawberries for the first time.
Crow's feet need not be blinders,
Arthritic fingers need not disqualify the quest
Any more than the deepest river need not inhibit the
    ferryman.
Life, liberty, and the pursuit of parts unknown
Need only a raft and a cable line,
The question, *What's on the other side?*
And the nose to go and see.

★★★

On August 6, 2012, NASA's Mars Science Laboratory landed the Mars rover, *Curiosity*. Its original two-year mission was to explore Martian climate and geology, specifically to determine if there were, and are, habitable conditions for life, including humans. It has succeeded beyond most NASA scientists' wildest dreams. As of March 2023, it was still operational, having added several new objectives to its work. Its mission has been extended indefinitely.[98]

A NASA panel selected the name *Curiosity* after a nationwide naming contest for students. The winner was twelve-year-old Clara Ma, a sixth-grader from Lenexa, Kansas. Here was what she had to say in her winning essay:

Curiosity is an everlasting flame that burns in everyone's mind. It makes me get out of bed in the morning and wonder what surprises life will throw at me that day. Curiosity is such a powerful force. Without it, we wouldn't be who we are today. Curiosity is the passion that drives us through our everyday lives. We have become explorers and scientists with our need to ask questions and to wonder.[99]

When I think of the word *curiosity*, my first images are of children, especially babies. Everything offers the potential for amazement and wonder to babies. Infants move from the breast or bottle to the jar of puréed food. They delight in taste and texture, even as they move into the world of solid foods. They study, in earnest, the new and different colors and shapes on their plates. More than just learning about the physical world around them, our babies and toddlers are also curious about their relational world. Sometimes, the interesting food on the plate becomes a game of call-and-response, wherein they will deposit said food on the floor and watch for the big person's reaction. A show we have seen many times. In an unusual variation on this dynamic, my youngest daughter wasn't into throwing food on the floor. Her tendency was to use french fries as a utensil for the salt she preferred much more than the fry itself. Sensing my disapproval, she would seek to do this surreptitiously.

An old aphorism derived from George Bernard Shaw is "youth is wasted on the young."[100] Understanding this is in reference to the hard-earned wisdom we may have in later years, the idea is we no longer possess the physical and emotional elasticity to fully benefit from our learnings. There are reasonable exceptions to this adage, a glaring one being curiosity.

Over the years, I have participated in numerous workshops and seminars on the practices of mindfulness. I remember doing a Mindfulness Based Stress Reduction course at my alma mater. I was able to fully engage and feel benefit from most of the exercises, with the exception of one. Taken from Thich Nhat Hanh, a Vietnamese Buddhist monk, this simple exercise involved deliberate time and experience with a raisin. We were instructed to spend time feeling its texture in our hands, observing its color and wrinkled, ridged form, before rubbing it across our lips and holding it to our noses to take in its scent. Next, we were to place it in our mouths, allowing it to sit, then roll it around without biting into it. Finally, we were to slowly bite into it, noticing the release of juices and flavor. We were to chew it for some ungodly number of times before swallowing it. I don't remember the number because I was nowhere near making it that long before just squashing it with my molars and gulping it down.

Surprise is an enzyme for curiosity—as is presence. Surprise comes mostly from the outside, although we do need to be in a receptive posture. Curiosity springs from within. Sometimes, our curiosity stems from the pure joy and stimulation of learning new things; other times, it is compelled from a state of need or lack. As we age, it is natural for us to accumulate experience and knowledge. This can, and does, create a bottleneck for our receptivity to surprise.

In today's age, we have access to nearly limitless information via the internet and social media. Plenty of jokes abound about us older folks having difficulty managing all this technology and needing to go find an eight-year-old grandchild or neighbor's kid to resolve our issue faster than a Rubik's Cube grandmaster. Noting this, many Third-Agers have actually assimilated to an appreciable degree and can scurry about the World Wide Web with relative ease. This has become both a blessing and a curse.

When our curiosity is whetted, for pleasure or need, YouTube videos stand at the ready. However, the other side of this digital coin is the aforementioned paradox of choice, along with the experiences of echo chambers and confirmation biases. Sometimes, we seek out information and feedback that confirms our established, and cherished, viewpoints. This is the antithesis of curiosity, and it is a rampant dynamic in our digital age.

We see and know all too well the negative effects of this. Conspiracy theories have greater traction than ever, given the tools of technology. Sociopolitical divides have become chasms, the impacts of which now show in historically apolitical areas of day-to-day life. Today, it's vital we reclaim curiosity to help us separate the informational wheat from chaff. We also still need to access curiosity in the lower and no-tech worlds. We still need physical touch. We need to get our hands dirty, like children creating mud pies or coloring chalk drawings on the sidewalk. Especially coming out of the dominant experience of the global pandemic, we need to travel to places around the world, or even to just a different county or state, to see and learn from those different from us.

I have had the pleasure of teaching classes at the nearby Osher Lifelong Learning Institute (OLLI) with North Carolina State University. Dating to 2001, the Bernard Osher Foundation has helped establish OLLIs at 120 universities and colleges across the United States. These institutes, for persons age fifty and older, offer a smorgasbord of curiosity-tapping courses ranging from organic gardening to the history of jazz to my course—exploring identity, meaning, relationships, and creativity in the Third Age. Many OLLIs also offer travel-related learning opportunities similar to Road Scholar.[101] It is a great pleasure to see Third-Agers remaining engaged in lifelong curiosity. It gives me great hope for our future.

An old joke that has quickly lost its 21st-century relevance is the one about men refusing to stop and ask for directions. While I will likely never be adept at holding food interminably in my mouth to learn more of its essence, I still do, on occasion, ignore or turn off my navigation system and drive unknown routes to experience heightened awareness and learn new pathways home.

★★★

Birdsong
What is it you are waiting for?
Why?
We have work to do.
The work of presence,
Of sitting and walking
Amidst the hued messengers of life.
The salutary sweet pea flower climbing the bowing trellis.
The glossy beetle rummaging along the brown, cracked
  earth.
Chevron geese carving through the salmon cloud tufts,
Streaking over silhouettes of silver queen stalks
Spent from the strain of the late summer harvest.
If we say we don't have the time,

We dismiss the universe,
We dismiss our loved ones,
And even more so our enemies.
Bells will toll when they will.
Whatever portal that lies before us,
It is nothing compared to the ground we currently attend.
If we act as if this moment is not worthy of our complete
  attention,
We dismiss ourselves.
At this moment,
There is a gospel chorus of birdsong
Just outside my window,
Beckoning me.
Offering lessons in pace and presence.
There is no delay worthy of my assent.

Come with me, and you'll be in a world of pure imagination.
—"Pure Imagination," written by Leslie Bricusse and Anthony Newly, from *Roald Dahl's Willy Wonka*

Gene Wilder's turn as the enigmatic, reclusive titan of children's candy in *Willy Wonka & the Chocolate Factory*, the film adaption of Roald Dahl's 1964 book *Charlie and the Chocolate Factory*, begins with singing the now-iconic song, "Pure Imagination." These transcendent lyrics and Wilder's lilting tenor have lured many chanteurs and chanteuses to follow suit in covering this classic song. We are often able to see archetypes—universal representations of certain basic personality or social dynamic types—in films and literature.[102] I started to look into the characters portrayed in the movie—confession: I have not reread Dahl's classic novel since childhood. It's readily apparent that Willy Wonka represents a few roles, including the magician, trickster, and overlord. Charlie, the hardscrabble and humble child of meager means, represents innocence and purity occluded in self-doubt. This is exacerbated by the experiences with his limiting grandparents, excepting Jack Albertson's encouraging character, Grandpa Joe. The remaining children visiting Wonka's factory are barely distinguishable from one another once you get past the window-dressing of their surface narrative. They are all portraying some variation on the theme of self-absorption. These various looks of selfishness all serve to ultimately exclude them from the literal and figurative grand prize: the keys to the kingdom. Charlie, next to his well-meaning but occasionally myopic grandfather, nearly loses the prize himself, given to his own lack of boldness and foresight.[103]

Like creativity, we often consider imagination to be a gift, inherently given to the lucky few. But I contend that a robust imagination is innate and available to us all. While natural, imagination is nonetheless like success in every other endeavor; it is 90 percent perspiration and 10 percent inspiration. The perspiration of imagination comes out of the inspiration and is passion aflame. Enacted interest at its three-dimensional peak. What do you love? Who do you love? It's damn near impossible to stimulate our imaginations over people, places, and things for which we are not interested.

In addition to passion, perspiration is also needed to battle self-limiting beliefs, those "protections" that offer us "safety" in the false gods of status and the material. Many of us have had our share of joys but have also absorbed much whittling worry, pain, and fatigue over the first halves of our lives. After age fifty, so many things, bland or benign, are prescribed, or worse, proscribed (read: banal) for us. Society reminds us of the boundaries of our senior-play area and tacitly rewards us for coloring within the senior lines. Some of us have so little left in reserve to respond to these soul-stifling circumstances we accept as the status quo. And we lose interest.

In Raleigh, the North Carolina Museum of Art (NCMA), a place of national repute, is a wellspring of imagination. More than just the work of the curators coordinating various shows and exhibits, this regional and national treasure has a bounty of offerings, shows, and classes ranging from the traditional arts for children of all ages to tai chi in the gardens to concerts and movies on the lawn. When I first discovered the NCMA back in the early 1990s, they had begun showing outdoor films on the windowless backside of the four-story, brick building. The staff would drape a massive white sheet from the roof over the back wall to serve as the giant screen projector. I was thoroughly impressed with this simple act of resourcefulness and imagination. What a great and effective cost-saving idea! The Audrey Hepburn film series they showed couldn't have had a finer venue.

In time, a major outdoor renovation was undertaken. The result of this was an intriguing combination of elements and landscapes, including a large, flat stone-and-metal map of North Carolina; a curved sandpit near the new, state-of-the-art screen projector; an amphitheater with an angled roof; a few curiously placed brick walls; and some shrubbery strategically placed to and fro. Certainly very passable to the casual eye. However, if one were to take a helicopter ride, or perhaps be aboard a commercial plane that was descending to the nearby Raleigh-Durham International Airport, one would see, in abundant clarity, the formation of the words *Picture This* made from the various items just mentioned. Ingenious. Imagination at the hands and minds of an environment that craves and exudes art.

If it feels like I'm a salesperson for the imagination fireworks rivaling the ubiquitous roadside tents that pop up every summer before July 4, I'll plead guilty as charged. Many of us have too much quality time ahead of us, too much untapped capacity and potential, too much joy left yet to know.

Leslie Bricusse and Anthony Newly wrote in their wonderous *Roald Dahl's Willy Wonka* song, "If you want to view paradise, simply look around and view it. Anything you want to, do it. Want to change [your] world? There's nothing to it." [104]

Words attributed to a man with roughly the same Imagination Quotient (ImQ) as you and I, Albert Einstein: "Imagination is more important than knowledge. Knowledge is limited. Imagination encircles the world."[105]

★★★

Hair
My mother used to sing with me.
She was alive when her throat was
Filled with the lyrics of Paul Simon
Or the soundtrack to *Hair*.
Not so much sweet as crisp,
A touch understated, but strong,
Like bamboo fiber while still green.

We would sing together, my mother and me,
And I would delight in her smile.
The way she leaned her head back,
Thick, dusty black hairs, moving en masse,
A herd of feral horses,
Deliberate, yet slightly askew
In its cadence with the chanteuse's selection.
It was beauty, my mom and her voice.

Her voice caressed her grandchildren.
Each one buoyed, womblike, in the soft lilt,
Of old Polish folk songs.
Gently pitched on the breeze of promise
That she would remain steadfast in song and love.
It was here in this aural alchemy,
That the divine spoke to unsuspicious eyes,
Of the third generation.

"Meet Me in Saint Louis" she sang, in response
To a Bailey White story I was reading to her.
Her smile was faint,
Barely perceptible on her thinly cracked lips.
The horses now wiry and gray, gaunt and lifeless.
Her bamboo dry and brittle.

I will not accept for posterity,
Those last pressed exhalations.
Though they were of my mother, they were not my mother.
She remains forever a song on the breeze,
Riding strong and free,
Sleek and strident on the feral mare.

I love music. Any kind of music. I love music. Just as long as it's groovy.
—"I Love Music" by The O'Jays,
written by Leon Huff and Kenny Gamble

Amy Grant, singer-songwriter and revered figure in both the Christian and crossover pop genres, recently played an intimate concert at her farm for roughly one thousand guests at the close of an event she was hosting. A friend of mine was there for the show and told me about a deeply moving experience within the event. Among others, Amy was interested in honoring United States military veterans. During the show, she shared a story about one particular veteran who played the cornet. Over the course of his military career, it was estimated he had played "Taps" more than one thousand times. More precisely, he played the one brief section of "Taps," the one piercing and universally associated with the moment of honoring the fallen in service of their country. This man eventually reached his pain-filled diminished return in this role. Struggling with significant PTSD, he retired from the military, gathered his collection of cornets, and promptly sold them. He would never play "Taps" again.

Then one day, about six years later, he was clearing things out of his mother's garage. And he came across one more old cornet ….

Amy continued the story by describing her daughter coming to her and saying, "Mom, who is that man out in the woods playing 'Taps'?" With tears in her eyes, in honor of all veterans and their loved ones, Amy pulled out her iPhone and shared an audio recording of this veteran playing "Taps" for the audience. There were audible gasps and barely suppressed cries of the veteran captured on the recording during the musical rests. To use an old, but most apt, phrase, there wasn't a dry eye in the place (Amy's farm).

It's a tough segue to go from The O'Jays to the disquietude of "Taps." But these are just two examples of the power of music on our hearts and minds. The history of music is replete with astonishing examples of genius and savants, from Libba Cotten and Mozart composing as young children, to Beethoven's masterful musical innovation through his loss of hearing, to kids with autism hearing complex pieces of music once and then sitting down at the piano and playing the compositions perfectly with no prior instruction or practice. Just the other day, I read an abstract detailing how the role and function of music is not diminished for folks with even advanced Alzheimer's and other dementias.[106] These anecdotes, and many more, point to the presence of neurological hardwiring. Research has pursued this neurological underpinning, innate in some form for each of us, by extending previous studies that confirmed the correlation of different musical patterns, tempos, and construction, with mood states.[107] Given music's ubiquity, researchers sought out indigenous peoples, confirming the absence of their exposure to different musical forms prevalent in the developed world. They replicated the previous studies and found unerring consistency in the high correlations between certain pieces of music and varied mood states.[108]

Mario is the cousin of my former partner and a gentle soul. In his early eighties, he lives a rich and peaceable life with his joyful wife Vivian. Their humble Berkley abode is immersed with walls of books on the inside and clusters of wildflowers on their small lot outside. And music. Mario and Vivian love music. I have a fond memory of visiting them and, not having my guitar with me, singing Billy Joel's "You're My Home" acapella while sitting around their kitchen table one late evening. When I finished, they both beamed and clapped with a hearty, "Encore!"

I recently received an email from Mario, saying he'd been diagnosed with Parkinson's. In typical Mario fashion, he took this news in stride and plainly switched over to talking about how much he enjoys my music. He asked if I would send him lyric sheets to my songs so he could sing along. He'd read about important treatment for Parkinson's, involving voice usage and control.[109] Included among the songs I sent Mario was "My Companion," an ode I wrote to music herself:

My Companion
In the early morning hour,
She's the heartbeat in my dreams
Sometimes she kisses me awake, and sometimes she screams
Voice so clear it haunts me, till I give her her just due
A lifetime conjoining, she's always seen me through
She travels so far and wide, she ages long and fine
She's just as at home with sweet iced tea, or the driest white
   wine
Never far from my mind, she's burrowed in my soul
Companion to the final breath, from the first my heart she
   stole
Trust is such a fluid creature, pathways so uneven
Seldom fickle is she, she rarely leaves me grieving
Word and tune together, Pan and wily shadow
Word and tune together, I will always follow
They will dance, we will dance too

I frequently talk with my clients about creating music playlists, not following general genre-related construction but rather being based on how it touches them emotionally. This makes it very personal. What specific songs inspire you when you are feeling low or facing a challenge? What music calms you? What songs help you to feel more industrious? I laugh at myself sometimes when I wake up wholly unmotivated on a Saturday morning, knowing the never-ending chore list awaits. Like the well-trained animal I am, all I have to do is put on music—you know, *that* particular music—and off I go to conquer the world, or, at least, the weeds in the backyard. If the neighbors get close enough to hear the sounds emanating from my pants pocket—I play my music from my smartphone sans earbuds—they are likely to hear Santana's "Europa," Jackson Browne's "Running On Empty," Steely Dan's "Peg," or most anything by Brandi Carlile, the Avett Brothers, or Amos Lee. If they caught me at another time in another context, they may very well hear Stevie Wonder or the Commodores.

Not limited to just music and our aural sensibilities, we all have senses with the potential to extend into the greater world and attach to the particular stimuli that enhances a desired mood or thought state. We are wired in a unique way with respect to which senses are more dominant for us. It serves us well to deliberately engage our particular sensory makeup. Bringing in the smells that remind us of the joyous parts of childhood; the soft or grainy fabrics, the feel of which drops our shoulders in times of stress; the body movements that restock our energy silos; the sights that excite us and focus us on the great task at hand. And for the pièce de résistance, the binding together of any desired experience with the perfect musical glue.

I just received another reply from Mario. He talked about the importance of physical exercise for his treatment. *So, Vivian and I are dancing wildly every night at home*, he wrote. He included a picture, the perfect embodiment of this couple's joyful and clear-eyed life perspective. They were smiling, cheek-to-cheek, holding hands in the pose of their favorite ballroom dance. He added in his note that he had also joined a Parkinson's choir. May we all know and inhabit Mario's spirit.

★★★

Play

Why so serious?
If Nero can fiddle while Rome burns,
Can I at least step back from the ledge of liminality
And whisper sweet nothings
In the inner ear of you, my child?
Could I find you hiding in the cupboard under the sink
Suppressing a giggle?
A wide-eyed gasp greeting me
Before I swat your forearm, turn and run,
Trusting you in the chase.
"You're it!"
It's true, you're it.
You are always it.
You are the chalky film covering my hands
And the moist beads on my forehead
As I finish the step, hop, plant, hop,
The hewn log bobbing in the clear stream
Carrying my dreams.
You are the updraft reducing my clay leaden feet.
You are the wet nurse, sating my arid and empty gut.
You're it. You've always been it.
Though I've ceded to the weight of burning Romes,
Decade over decade.
You waited in impish purity,
With my blotchy and creased hand reaching for the cupboard
  handle.
You're it.

Play is never far from the impress of the creative drive,
never far from the happiness of discovery.
—MARY OLIVER, *UPSTREAM*

Hunter "Patch" Adams is a medical doctor, author, social activist, and cofounder of the Gesundheit! Institute. Perhaps most importantly, he is a clown. His GO!CLOWNS missions bring light and healing to countless communities across the globe. These troupes of clowns perform; offer "playshops" to children in art, music, and theater; and assist with carpentry, painting, and other needed services in distressed communities.[110]

His story was adapted for the big screen, with Robin Williams giving his take on who this mythic figure is. In the movie *Patch Adams*, the lead character starts out in a psychiatric hospital, overwrought with suicidal depression. His roommate Rudy, marvelously played by Michael Jeter, needs to use the bathroom in the middle of the night. He is trapped on his bed, being dogged and distressed by the marauding, pernicious squirrels of his psychosis. Seeing Rudy terrified and stricken by the gnawing hallucinations, Patch jumps into action, joining his roommate in vanquishing the vehement vermin. He does so through the vehicle of play. Given the harshness and violence of Rudy's experience, it certainly doesn't feel like play. It feels like life or death to Rudy, and Patch approaches it with total focus and respect.

It is a remarkable scene that sets up the rest of the movie, serving as the clarion event by which Patch realizes his calling in life: helping others in distress. He chooses the traditional route of medical school and soon comes to recognize the high import of play, laughter, and frivolity in everyone's healing. This flies in the face of the moribund faculty and his fellow classmates, including his roommate Mitch, astutely crafted by Phillip Seymour Hoffman. Throughout the movie, we see the interweaving of play and lightness with tragedy and sorrow. A modern manifestation of the Melpomene and Thalia (tragedy and comedy) masks of early Greek theater.[111]

Sometimes play dwells in the space of generative joy, sometimes it is in direct response to life's injuries and malignancies, and sometimes it involves risk.

Despite the challenges of my youth—or, perhaps, because of them?—I was a child of mirth, merriment, and mischief. This temperament and evolving worldview allowed me a pathway to discovery: learning the auguries of relationships, man-made systems, and, at the most foundational, the natural world. As a function of this, I far and away led my family in hospital ER visits. During our 1978 summer trip, one such occasion unfolded, culminating in a trip to a small clinic a half-hour ride away from our cabin rental in Woolwine, a small unincorporated community in the foothills of Southern Virginia.

Following an afternoon of catching grasshoppers and collecting them in a small instant-coffee jar, my brother Lee and I sauntered off down a long, winding trail to the Smith River, a good-sized tributary of the Dan River, to go trout fishing. Lee had his temporary fishing license, and I was along for the adventure, mostly wading out into the middle of the cold mountain water. I would deftly open the jar lid and corral one of the grasshoppers without losing the rest and hand it to Lee to use as bait. It wasn't long before our event was irretrievably disrupted. I had adjusted my stance in the roughly two-to-three feet of water and slipped on a mossy riverbed rock. Falling backward, my natural instinct was to fling my arms behind to catch my fall. All well and good ... unless you are holding a glass jar, which, of course, I was.

The water was quite cold and brisk with some flow to it. These factors perhaps blunted the reality that I had severely cut my left hand in two places. I gathered myself to stand again, and as I lifted my arms out of the stream, I noticed the gushing blood. I reacted by thrusting my hand back into the water, as if that would somehow resolve the situation. I then quickly focused and realized I needed to apply pressure with my other hand and raise the wound above my head. Both Lee and I were rather matter-of-fact about the situation. I don't remember which one of us said, "Well, let's go."

About an hour later, I was sitting in the clinic chair, recounting the tale for the third or fourth time while the doctor stitched closed the two deep gashes in my hand. Doing so, I was reminded of my first trip to the ER at age six.

After the close of my baby sister Beth's baptism, when leaving the church, a family-friend challenged me to a race to my grandmother's '68 Dodge Polara. The car handles in those days were solid metal protrusions, waiting invitations for calamity. As we closed in, neck-and-neck on the de facto finish line, we stumbled into one another. I fell forward and planted my left eyebrow and eye socket squarely on said car handle. Unaware I was badly hurt, and thinking I was just sweating from the humid Milwaukee summer air, I climbed into the backseat. It was only when I glanced in the rearview mirror and saw the left half of my face covered in deep-red blood that I realized I might have a problem.

Coming back to the Woolwine trip, the doctor told me how very fortunate I was that there was no tendon or ligament damage and I didn't nick an artery. He wrapped the wound in gauze and instructed me to limit my activity and keep my hand dry. At the risk of typecasting, saying this to a thirteen-year-old adventuresome boy is akin to talking to the wall ... mostly.

In my mind, I was quite cognizant of the directive to keep the wound dry. This would be evidenced the next day when Lee and I went tubing in the same river. I was conscientious of keeping my bandaged left hand elevated and just using my right hand and lower legs to steer as the river carried us forward. This instruction was further put to the test when Lee and I saw a water moccasin sunning on a nearby rock on the riverbank. We had been enjoying a fairly lazy float when we decided it would be interesting and fun to throw small rocks at the snake, who subsequently slipped into the water. Next, without particular panic, we started thrashing forward with available appendages to get away from the snake. I remember still keeping my left hand up, leveraging my butt up out of the water so as to not get bitten there, and trying to use only my legs and right hand to scoot down the river. A foolish escapade indeed for two boys to do but one that sparked plenty of laughter during and after our successful escape.

Play takes many forms. With respect to Mary Oliver's words, it is a primary handmaiden of creativity and discovery.[112] As such, it must include a significant element of spontaneity. Play is open and vulnerable and has the most natural internal feedback loop. In its purest form, it is uninhibited, free from societal and familial conditioning and layering, and thus, it escapes the distortion and bastardization of the authentic. To play is to be present. It doesn't have to be an escapade; it can be solely an act of joy. But because it will often intersect with the outside world, it will, at times, include risk and result in pain, physical or emotional. The longer we live, the more unavoidable it is for us to accrue more hurts, which can easily make us more cautious. This can have the unfortunate limiting effect of dampening our natural capacities for play.

Many nonhuman mammals model a more natural expression of play as a means of exploring their environments and the other members of their communities. Ever watch two otters manifest unbridled joy as they scurry about their habitat at the zoo? Another example is sheep. Contrary to popular opinion, sheep are neither stupid nor helpless. Each has its own unique personality, and they are often quite joy-filled and playful. I like to imagine this was true for Baarack, the wayward sheep discovered in early 2021 in a forest north of Melbourne, Australia. Baarack was found after an undetermined, but lengthy, amount of time with an astounding seventy-five pounds of wool weighing him down and occluding his vision. Sheep need regular shearing to remain healthy. Baarack's fleece was matted with feces and urine, keeping him at risk for infections. Grit and debris were lodged between his corneas and eyelids, leading to ulcers. Despite the weighty wool, Baarack was actually underweight after being sheared. A healthy wool also helps the animal to better control its body temperature. If Baarack began his ordeal in search of adventure, he must have eventually been burdened by loneliness and physical distress.[113]

In my time with many Third-Agers, I've seen all manner of response to the accrual of lifetime hurts. Predictably, some folks wear their hurts like Baarack. Starting life on a more uninhibited track, these folks succumb over time to the vagaries and slights of life and relationships. Some experience powerful, exacting trauma. Either way, they arrive at this time of life with psychic burden and infection.

In the movie mentioned earlier, Patch Adams met a girl who was buried in mis-considered, protective wool. This was, in reality, a platonic, male friend of his, rescripted by Hollywood for the romantic angle and intrigue. Patch was drawn to her, compelled to help her discover his world of play and social engagement. Through persistence and an uneven trajectory, she did indeed come to this generative view. Despite the further tragedy that followed, Patch was able to continue his play-filled journey.[114]

Some Third-Agers evolve along a different path, sloughing off the excess wool of judgment and expectation. These folks have what feels like a natural buoyancy, an ability to respond to life's slings and arrows with aplomb. While genetics may play a fortunate role for these life-embracers, I suspect they've arrived at, and maintained, this resilience through intention and courage in the face of travail and adversity.

Among and amidst the paths of creativity necessary for our well-being throughout life, play feels particularly important. Shearing off—or, at least, regulating—the woolen hurts of our cumulative years is the perpetual prerequisite and purview of play.

***

Today
Join me for the day.
We'll start in the dandelion field,
Blowing a thousand wishes upon the breeze,
Watching snow fall in June.
We'll sling stones, skipping across the waiting lake,
And coo with the mourning doves perched on the loblolly
  branch above.
Call and response.

Next, we'll swivel inelegant hips
In the losing effort to keep hoops waisted,
Laughing and gasping for air
Before sitting cross-legged on the baked red ground
Telling our favorite secrets,
One for each four-leaf clover we found in the nearby grass.
Fortune and release.

Before night falls
We'll stop by the neighbor's apiary
And stare in still wonder as the honeybees
Circle our heads and crawl over our outstretched hands,
Each of us curious and light,
Knowing beyond species that we are kindred.
Touch and pause.

With the dappled moon, ascending and full,
We'll settle on the porch swing
And sway in the creaking cadence,
The day's warmth dissolving into the cool night air.
We have been about the work of now,
Breathing, drinking, touching, moving, being.
Here and eternal.

★★★

What are the animals of your dreams?
Courage is the fiercest winged beast I know.
It beckons me, dares me, to climb its back
And press my aroused grip into its taut flesh
While we rise to see new lands,
The dirt of Nebuchadnezzar in its mouth,
The exhale of one trillion stars in its nostrils.

There is no promise of peace,
No words of soft comfort,
Only the commission of life.
That is, to see what is before me,
To state what is upon me,
To choose its name.

You say you can't create something original? Don't worry about it.
Make a cup of clay so your brother [or sister] can drink.

—Rumi

Another pillar in the general fields of neurobiology and cognitive-behavioral psychology is the work around learned helplessness and attribution theory. Learned helplessness arose out of some troubling trials with dogs by the prominent psychologist Martin Seligman and his colleagues in the late 1960s. In the experiments, the dogs were repeatedly shocked without any discernible way to escape the painful experience. Even after the impediment to their escape was removed, many of the dogs remained passive to the opportunity to free themselves from the distressing shock. Through the repeated events, the dogs had acquired a learned state of helplessness. They resigned themselves to ongoing pain.[115]

Aside from the hard ethical implications of these experiments, the studies were intended to find a window into the causes of depression, a condition that has a devastating impact on millions of persons every year, including seniors. Today, depression annually affects around six million individuals age sixty-five and older in the United States. Common drivers for this include any number of loss experiences, from the deaths of loved ones to declining health, purpose, mobility, autonomy, and financial resources, to name but a few.[116] This has certainly been exacerbated through the time of the COVID-19 pandemic. To frame this in a broader context, it is about the loss of control. Seligman and his colleagues continued their work using attribution theory later in the 1970s. Attribution theory speaks to the motivation of humans to assign cause to their actions and behaviors. It gives a further delineation to the perspective about loss of control, looking at three scales: internal/external, stable/unstable, and global/specific. They posited that people who were more likely to attribute negative events to internal, stable, and global causes were more likely to become depressed as compared to folks at the other end of the scales.[117]

Over the past few decades, advances in neuroscience have inverted the original theory, suggesting the brain's default state is to assume that control is not present, and *helpfulness* is actually learned.[118] While it feels ominous to consider an overarching atmosphere of no control, it feels hopeful to me to consider I can *learn* pathways to peace and ground.

Additional insights are continuing in the intermingling fields of psychology and neurology. In more practical and applied terms, how we consider our lot in life—and, more specifically, our present station—goes supremely far in contributing to our choices and actions, which, in turn, reinforce our perspective. It's a feedback loop, with momentum begetting momentum, we can put our hands and minds on.

One particular area of clinical research that looks at intervening in physical and social ways to positively impact our minds is with volunteerism. To be clear, the primary point of volunteering is not to help ourselves. It is for the betterment of someone or something outside ourselves, and yet, the current research shows clear emotional and mental health benefits to all involved. Indeed, some research specifically shows that persons who start out with lower levels of well-being may get an even bigger boost from volunteering.[119]

A classic win-win.

When I think of the embodiment of learned *helpfulness*, Ruth Bader Ginsberg—a.k.a. RBG—is one of the first persons to come to mind. Though standing five foot one, RBG was a towering figure. Across the whole of her life, she represented resilience in the face of adversity. Early family deaths, blazing trails for women through law school and in arguing before the Supreme Court, supporting her husband while both were in law school and he was wrangling with cancer, these are but a few of the remarkable responses she had to adversity over the course of her inspiring life. This culminated over the last portion of her twenty-seven-year Supreme Court Justice tenure as she mounted her own steadfast campaign against pancreatic cancer. An enduring image of RBG is one of when she was doing lat pulldowns with her personal trainer. During her daily morning workout, she donned a sweatshirt with the phrase "Super Diva."

When asked how she would like to be remembered, RBG replied, "[As] someone who used whatever talent she had to do her work to the very best of her ability. And to help repair tears in her society, to make things a little better through the use of whatever ability she has. To do something, as my colleague David Souter would say, outside myself. 'Cause I've gotten much more satisfaction for the things that I've done for which I was not paid."[120]

My friend Sharon is a staunch RBG devotee. To know Sharon's story is to have a better appreciation for her RBG admiration. Hailing from central Virginia, she marshalled the courage to leave an abusive marriage, with her two young sons, and migrate to North Carolina. Over many years of illness and vigor, joy and broken relationships, and, most of all, steadfast wonder, Sharon has persevered. A number of years ago, she successfully overcame breast cancer. More recently, she had a life-threatening bout with a common and typically benign bacteria that attacked her liver. In response to this, during her three-week stay in the hospital, Sharon used a visualization to help with her healing. She eventually shared this visualization in a letter she sent to RBG. Here's a portion of the letter:

I am a firm believer in the power of laughter! One late afternoon, I was having a test done in the hospital, and I remembered Gilda Radner and her struggles with cancer. I remembered that in her book, she mentioned her visualization of dancing and stomping out her cancer cells. I am not entirely sure this is accurate, since I read the book a number of years ago, but that is the memory that prompted me to think I needed a visualization of my own! When I returned to my room, my son and his friend were there. We chatted about all sorts of things, including you! Then I told them I needed help brainstorming a visualization to crush out the bacteria. Without a pause, my son's friend said, "You and Ruth Bader Ginsberg can use gavels and smash the bacteria!" It was the PERFECT visualization! I used it from then on, many times a day! A few days later, she also said we could be yelling while smashing the bacteria, "You're unconstitutional!"

Although her recovery continued along a slow, uneven trajectory, Sharon did indeed steady her way back to health. Laughter and RBG-inspired fortitude were every part the equals to her rest and antibiotic IV drips.

I can attest to Sharon's laughter. I'm not sure I have ever had a conversation with her where laughter was absent. It is her superpower. That and her clarity about living simply with wonder and gratitude and a love and service for all things alive. Throughout her trials, if you dropped into Sharon's world at any given time, you would see her using her skills to read picture books to children during church services; acting in a quirky, local indie film; sharing creepy-crawlies with visitors at the State Museum of Natural Science's annual Bugfest; or volunteering at the North Carolina Reading Service, a non-profit that helps connect visually, and print-impaired persons with the greater community via audio recordings of newspapers, magazine articles, and books read by volunteers. I've had the pleasure of watching Sharon in this element, donning oversized headphones, working the sea of knobs on the soundboard, and flashing her signature smile while reading from one of my earlier books.

Looking at Sharon's preferred activities, it comes as no surprise that she worked in a university library. After seventeen years, with her latest job at North Carolina State University, Sharon is very close to retiring. When she does, she wants to sell her modest suburban home and "go live in a room somewhere." This is not a statement of defeat or depression, though it appears to rub against one of the prevailing interests many hold when retiring: to rest in the material abundance for which we've worked so long and hard. In fairness, there is nothing inherently wrong with that mind state. What matters is the lens through which we view our circumstances and choices. If we craft a lens of gratitude, then any choice we make about how to live in our post-career years will surely be uplifted by joy.

Sharon's interest to live simply is another prevailing mind state for Third-Agers. One of her sons is in Colorado, the other in Maryland. She is in the process of decluttering her home, recklessly and lavishly tossing over jetsam to better buoy her voyage to her next destination, likely near one of her sons. Coming through and out of her recent serious illness and into the time of the global pandemic impeded Sharon's quest to prepare her home for sale. She has confessed to moments of becoming overwhelmed by the whole process.

I shared with her the fun urban legend of someone mailing a jeep home from World War II, piece by piece. This was later reenacted in an episode of *M*A*S*H* Sharon found and watched.[121] Since then, Sharon has told me how helpful this imagery was on several occasions for her to manage the unmanageable. She keeps mailing jeep parts home.

So there Sharon is, right as rain in her dogged pursuit of trekking toward retirement and the simple life while still in the midst of the COVID-19 pandemic when ... she had to have a total knee replacement. Another impediment in the road. Another gangly piece of jeep to figure out how to mail home. How did Sharon handle this latest hurdle? With understandable ardor, grind, pain, exhaustion ... and laughter. A fitting picture to the whole of this experience is Sharon lying supine on the table in the physical therapy office, singing sea shanties while they worked on her knee, inspiring other patients present to join in.

A few years before the pandemic, Sharon took up juggling. She laughs when she bests her previous record for number of successful rotations without a drop. She laughs when she has a drop after only a few turns. She has shared with me that on several occasions, when the stress of work was reaching its apex, she would go outside and juggle. The literal quality and benefit of the focus this requires is a great antidote to stress. Similarly, the metaphorical value of seeking to hold a modicum of control and the reflexive ability to laugh when that control crumbles is priceless.

Sharon has come to this time in her life, as most of us do, through challenge and tumult—broken family and friend relationships, grinding times of and through illness. But through and beyond these experiences, Sharon has chosen joy. In the face of often unavoidable depression that accompanies these dark times, she kept reaching for gratitude. She continues to learn *helpfulness*. The path has been uneven, but in the spirit of RBG, one of the steadfast anchors for Sharon has been the giving of herself and her gifts to others. That and her superpower: laughter.

★★★

Laughing Together
Laugh with me
And we'll drink life's marrow as it greases our chins,
And fall into a deep, sated slumber

Laugh at me
And my lungs will seize with the burn of arctic air,
Coughing up almond-tinted phlegm

Laugh with me
And I'll know you carry in your hand fresh green mullein
Opening me to my own course

Laugh at me
And you'll tell me my place amidst the menagerie of life
Is but a fleck of mica to cleave and carry away

Laugh with me
And you'll lift the labored veil on my loneliness,
Exposing me to light and love

Laugh at me
And the pages of my life will yellow and seep over the
  fading font,
Story languishing, opportunity lost

Laugh with me
And we will mount James Wright's horses, now pegasi,
Blessed to fly into the deep blue sea above the world

Allow me to lead, remind me that I can
And I'll take my rightful place as your fellow heir
Under the starry canopy of kind connection
Laughing together.

★★★

In the 1990s, every Monday night, a quirky, out-of-the-box comedy drama was consistently on my TV set. *Northern Exposure*, set in a fictional, at turns bucolic and biting, Alaskan town burst onto the scripted show landscape with an originality and irreverence that garnered it much acclaim and awards. It was listed as a drama, but it was rife with subtle, offbeat humor, individualized for each cast of characters. I absolutely loved this show.

In the final episode of season two, the absurdity was in high form. Maggie, an independent, self-made woman who has endured a series of statistically unimaginable situations, namely having several boyfriends die in freak accidents, has yet to experience one more. She skittishly has been in a relationship with Rick, another Alaskan bush pilot, and is slowly coming to think her "curse" has been lifted when word comes to her that he too, has been killed. This time, the culprit was debris from a rogue satellite falling back to Earth. It struck him while he was relaxing by the campfire in the backcountry.

In a subsequent scene, the town gathers for the funeral in a small church. Chris Stevens, the town's DJ and general raconteur, is set to deliver a eulogy. There is an open casket, of necessity, because the satellite debris has fused with the body, leaving metal prongs jutting out several feet. During a reverent pause, someone in the gathering snickers, and soon, the floodgates have been opened. The whole church, including Chris who's standing at the pulpit, roars at the pure absurdity of it all.

Here's a bit of this episode's dialogue from two other droll characters:

Ruth-Anne: Reminds me of Abe Kellogg. When he got caught in the machinery in the cannery.

Holling Vincoeur: They had to recall a hundred cases of salmon.

Ruth-Anne: I'll never forget that funeral, watching them lower all those itty bitty cans into the ground.[122]

Continuing on the theme of humor and laughter, I have watched and experienced my HQ (humor quotient) modulate and reform. In my early years, I was the quintessential class clown. Sharon Wegscheider-Cruse, an addictions expert who coined certain names for clearly identifiable roles and patterns in family addictions, called this the "mascot."[123] By and large, my approach was self-deprecating, falling on my own comic sword as a means of hiding in plain sight. This penchant's half-life seemed spent by the time I finished college and ventured into the waiting world beyond my family. At a few different points, I wondered if I had lost my HQ altogether. Challenging experiences in life can have that effect for some of us. For others, humor becomes and sustains as the main go-to in times of strife. Certainly, the longer we live, the fuller our buckets are with the brackish water of joy and heartache.

Humor can be joyful, the spontaneous expressions of babies.

Humor can be cute, the goofy actions of our pets.

Humor can be self-deprecating, the lightness we bring to some misstep that reminds us it's really no big deal in the grander scheme of life.

Much humor comes from familiarity, our relating to another's experience. This is the "laughing with" quality of humor. We do need to take care in these instances for the needs and sensitivities of the others who are directly involved.

Certain sounds are funny. Certain faces and images, when intended, are funny. Words and names can be funny. I remember listening to the call-in radio show *Car Talk* one Saturday many years ago. The show was famous for the banter and ribbing between the two brothers hosting the show, Tom and Ray Magliozzi. It was equally, if not more, famous for Tom's self-deprecation and big, boisterous laugh. In this particular episode, an Indian gentleman called in and introduced himself. His name had repeating, looping lilts, and it immediately sent Tom into uproarious laughter that took several minutes to quell. It is certainly possible the man could have been offended by this. It didn't appear so given the ensuing conversation, which included Tom's apology.[124]

Authentic humor is always creative and often spontaneous. Creativity isn't always funny. As shared earlier, creativity includes problem-solving and broader experiences of generativity. But funny is always creative.

Humor can be dark, a way to release the fierce rip current that is a very real and ominous threat to our well-being. This is often tied to the absurdities of life, the bread and butter of *Northern Exposure*, those times and events that are wildly out of our control. It is here, in using humor to deal with pain, we walk a potentially fine line with inauthenticity. The tears of a clown may buoy and sustain the person, or they may inhibit the individual from dealing with, recovering from, and growing out of the trauma. Any time humor is created out of the hard misfortune of another, it is unhealthy for all involved. Sarcasm is a ripe candidate for this inauthenticity.

By the time we reach our Third Age, we've logged many, many miles and, hopefully, laughed through quite a few. By this time, it's likely we've, intentionally or not, calibrated our HQ to some relatively fixed point on the scale. And furthering the downward pressure is our uneven experience of increasing losses as we age. The good news is, if our HQs are lower than we'd like, we have the gift and graft of neuroplasticity to help us rejigger our funny bones. If we are partnered at this time, given the complexities and challenges of any and every relationship, as noted in the "Tendrils" section, it is essential we tend to the Couple HQ—the couple's shared patterns of lightness, banter, and release that serve as glue and balm for the relationship. If we are long-term partnered, we may be in a nice groove, a deep knowing of each other across many areas. No question that a healthy Couple HQ would serve each in the needed resilience for certain aspects of the aging process. It's also possible there is an evolution, an arc to one or both persons' HQ characters. This is highly unlikely to happen in a vacuum, thus, if there are experiences that alter one or both individuals' humor proclivities, this will likely be known over a period of time and, in the best outcomes, accounted for and adjusted to via ongoing and healthy dialogue.

I certainly don't laugh as often as I did in my youth, and in a few respects, that is a good thing. But, in my estimation, I don't laugh as much as I should or could. This is a present and most-relevant conversation with my love Heather. She has a freer relationship with humor that serves her well. I do want to laugh more. Perhaps I, or we, should go back and rewatch *Northern Exposure*.

★★★

Beauty
Wander amidst the fetid dank alley
Where broken glass and a drunk's piss
Pool in cobblestone crevices,
He's there in the rosy pink fingers
Of the brown boy bringing day-old bread
To consumptive mouths

Stand next to the open window
The hanging flower box still lauding
Half-petaled red geranium heads,
She's there in the honeyed decibel drop
Of the wife's call to remember
The couple's gentle succor

Peer into the dark sky's milky spray
Of unbound stars through the telescope's lens
Time frozen, time in gaseous irreverence,
She's there in the silent stillness
Of the Earth's steady rotation
To the pastel dawn's calling

Walk through a field's dingy white riot,
Having escaped suburbia's proper poison pith,
He's there, in the cracked, ashen pucker
Of the migrant's son's mouth
Blowing blessings and dandelion seeds
On the moist morning breeze

Somewhere between the mountains and the rocky coast
lies a forest of pristine green, forgotten by most.
Deep in this forest is a secret place
with 10 golden seeds at the end of a maze.
They were hidden by five giant forest trolls
protecting each part of the forest so old.
It was told that the trolls spoke the tongue of the trees
and had sworn to protect them from war and disease.
Birk had roots. Røskva was wide as the trunks.
Gro was like the leaves, breathing life with her lungs.
Søren, like branches, would wave in the wind,
and Lilja, like the flowers, each year would spring.
—From "Guardian of the Seeds"
by Thomas Dambo

Thomas Dambo is a Danish artist who describes himself as a "recycle art activist." From an early age, he was known to scavenge his neighborhood, in search of discarded or neglected scraps of wood to transform into works of beauty. He is now considered to be one of the world's leading recycled-materials artists, and his beloved trolls can be found worldwide, touting the beauty and essence of conservation and global connection.[125]

Thanks to Thomas Dambo, I have a new fascination with trolls. Recently, on a trip to New England with Heather, we made plans to go to the Coastal Maine Botanical Gardens. One of my interests in going was to see the five giant trolls subtly positioned throughout the Gardens. These larger than (human) life-sized creatures did not disappoint. Trolls, deriving from ancient Nordic traditions, were considered to be monstrous and ugly and possessing magical, primarily malevolent, powers. This was before DreamWorks gave them a modern makeover in animated films, turning them into small, relatable, cuddly caricatures. For my interests, I prefer Dambo's treatment. His creations are physically imposing and remain conventionally aesthetically challenging, but along with their accompanying stories and missions, you are drawn to an ethereal and quiet beauty for each one.

As described on the Coastal Maine Botanical Gardens website: "With a belief that beauty can be found anywhere—especially in unexplored regions of our own backyards—his trolls are always hidden, but the diligent seeker will soon find them 'hidden' in plain sight."[126]

Reading the accompanying bios and mission narratives of each troll and taking in their quiescent beauty, I found myself extending and expanding the qualities that manifest their charm and allure. In their roles as guardians of the seeds and protectors of the trees, I see:

Røskva, who stands for trunks, grows taller and wider with each season, and remembers everything, represents beauty as growth. Beauty is generative. This does not always mean adding more. There certainly are times when we add via subtraction. But often, the integration of life experiences results in growth that is beauty.

Lilja, who holds the scent of the flowers, is still a child, and loves the colors of bees and butterflies, represents beauty as vibrancy. This is the closest to framing beauty as a visual aesthetic. Short of being limited to a material character, vibrancy is an active energy. It is the manifestation of an attitude, an outlook that says, "You matter and so do I."

Birk, who holds the roots, is the wisest, listens to the whispers of the soil, and tells stories to all the other forest creatures, represents beauty as tradition. The integrated product of experience, wisdom, is beautiful. The familiar, the revered, the honoring of the ways of those who came before us. The receiving of their gifts of legacy.

Søren, who sticks up for the branches, is always dreaming and searching, and loves to dance, represents beauty as curiosity. This is the beauty of youthfulness, not age-dependent or -defined, but the spirit of discovery which brings a beauty in fulfillment.

Gro, who smiles with the leaves, wanders about tending to her friends, and creates feasts for the forest family with a handful of sunbeams and raindrops, represents beauty as *compassion*. The penultimate action representing the best of our species.[127]

Aesthetics matter. I'm not interested in downplaying the value and importance of sensory-based beauty. But external beauty decamped from an inner wellspring is vapid and shallow and, ultimately, ephemera. Beauty as ephemera is actually a reference to an inauthentic beauty. It is quite easy to see the conditioning forces at work in our societies, assigning greater status to people and things that hold and exemplify a certain, and ultimately arbitrary, standard. For many of us, as we age, we are less able to meet and sustain these external standards, if ever we were. And the double standards. Oh, the double standards. Not the least of which is judgment of women so harshly as they age. Whereas men who are gray and creviced are viewed as regal and wise, the women who are gray and creviced are viewed as haggard and crone-like.

The issue of beauty as we age offers an important opportunity to examine how we feel about ourselves and the world around us. Given the societal imprint, it is understandable there are strong ties to our sense of identity. We may reach backward for the beauty of our youth via plastic surgery, hair implants, or dyes. We may unwittingly absorb the messaging that would diminish our sense of self due to our changing appearance over time. Coming through these experiences, how do we find a better access into authentic beauty that is not overly defined by our physical attributes?

In the movie *Forrest Gump*, Tom Hanks's lead character is considered to be slow-witted by many, yet he is amazingly accomplished over the course of his life. He is asked on several occasions if he is stupid, to which he replies, "Mama says, 'Stupid is as stupid does.'"[128] The implication here is that one's actions should be the determinant, not one's IQ. Borrowing from this idea, I would offer that "beauty is as beauty does." The verb creates the noun. In other words, it is how I carry and extend myself, not my two-dimensional physical appearance, that creates beauty. The aesthetic follows the function.

The attributes I assigned to each of Dambo's trolls are but a few of the "behaviors" that can be the source and expression of beauty. There is beauty in growth and vibrancy. In tradition and curiosity and compassion. I would go further in saying where there is an authentic sense of meaning or purpose (the function), there is always beauty (the aesthetic).

In my mid-twenties, I was part of a professional panel doing a test run on a new school curriculum that sought to use a Paideia Socratic seminar to facilitate greater critical thinking with students. We were to discuss the prompt, "As humans, are we born inherently good or inherently evil?" Not surprisingly, the debate pinged and wove in and through discussion of psychology, religion, and neurophysiology. I was absorbing most of the conversation before raising another consideration: "What if we are born as blank slates, tabula rasa?" In an unintentionally typical Socratic form, I was raising the question without presuming to know the answer.

The term *tabula rasa*, as a philosophical construct, has been around since the days of Aristotle, being more formally assigned in the late 1600s by the British philosopher John Locke.[129] While still not knowing with any certainty the answer to the original question, I have substantially moved in one particular direction, largely ruling out the tabula rasa postulate. For me, the key insight resides in the dynamic of creativity. We are fundamentally born as creative, generative beings. We manifest creativity, which starts from the inside and then responds to, or aligns with, the world around us. And it is beautiful. Beauty as Røskva, Lilja, Birk, Søren, and Gro. Beauty as You. Beauty as Me.

We still have the haranguing question to answer regarding destruction and malevolence in the world. We see so much violence and enmity, it is easy to be overwhelmed. My understanding through the lens of psychology and neurophysiology is pure evil in the form of severe conditions, such as sociopathy and psychopathy, is uncommon. What is far more common is the poor adaptation to the challenges and stressors of life that expose us to unhealthy anxieties and prompt us to make ugly choices that hurt others and ourselves. So, on a practical level, it appears the high majority of us are a mixture of beauty and the grotesque. Despite this presentation, I still see our underlying core as creative. It is the hard life experiences that can distort and inhibit what is natural. But often these hard life experiences are also the germ for some of life's greatest art, traditional and non.

We are designed to create. We can create beauty or destruction and, over time, do both. But what is our aggregate? I came across a quote from my favorite visual artist Vincent Van Gogh, a man whose place in history is poignantly marked by his creation of beauty over and beyond his deep, ugly personal darkness: "I feel there's nothing truly more artistic than loving people."[130]

I love these words and would presume to substitute the word *beautiful* for *artistic*. And as for the word *loving*, is it an adjective, a verb, or both?

Irrespective of our age and physical changes, we are lifelong creators. We retain the capacity for beauty throughout our lives.

EPILOGUE: TREES

In the '70s, Elton John and Bernie Taupin wrote "Your Song," a Top 10 hit in several countries, one of many for the inimitable songwriting team. The story of the creation of this song follows an oft repeated newsworthy account. They wrote the song in twenty minutes, as Taupin recounts, "on a grubby piece of exercise paper, sitting at the kitchen table."[131]

There is a common question when considering many works of art, particularly with music, poetry, and literature: "How long did it take you to write this?" It strikes me as odd that, largely in the industrialized world, we single out time, expedited and compressed, as virtuous. I intellectually understand this from a free-market economy perspective. Time is money. The more I can produce in shorter time increments, the greater the return. But why, and how, does this translate to the rest of our experiences, notably the world of art and relationships?

I can follow that the "how long" question may have as its original intent to honor brilliance and see creativity in its pure form. But time commodified distorts and bastardizes experience. It has no real meaning in the life of art and relationships. A piece may take two minutes or twenty years to be materially composed. Equally, a relationship may come into fullness in thirty minutes or thirty years. In truth, like any of my songs, poems, or books, it has taken me the length of my life to write this book. Anything you or I do has reach and supply going back the length of our lives. But the question of time is embedded in our homes and hearts. And as we move further toward the conclusion of our place in this life and world, how do we engage time?

Paul and Frances Allred lived behind us when my family first moved to my boyhood home in Oak Ridge. Home to mostly tobacco fields, cow pastures, and clusters of modest ranch houses, Oak Ridge felt like a time apart from the rest of the world—at least, it did to this mop-headed boy of fanciful imagination and more than a touch of mischievousness. The Allreds had retired many years before and enjoyed the easy cadence of Oak Ridge life. Paul collected arrowheads and other Native-American tools found on the local lands. He took a special interest in sharing this passion with Lee and me. On occasional spring mornings, he would take us to various newly plowed fields to hunt for arrowheads before the crops had been planted. This was but one of many out-of-time childhood experiences for me, further punctuated upon finding one of these precious stones.

The adventures of that young boy soon gave way to adolescence and participation in some of its proscribed rites. Adolescence segued into the independence and exploration of young-adult university life, which, in turn, begot the joys and toils of family and career. Today, my vocation in psychology and counseling has stretched to over thirty years. Now, as I speak blessings to both my daughters—my oldest embarking on graduate school in social work, and my youngest on her way into her undergraduate world away from home—I remember their earlier years and am reminded of my own youth. As is often the case, many artifacts of our youth, including my small, ruddy collection of arrowheads, were lost along the way. But the memories remain.

As I am traversing yet another threshold along the linear time continuum most of us unwittingly subscribe to, I'm choosing to say "yes" to time. Not in the aforementioned linearity, wherein time is a quantification, nor in the culturally carved construct that our western, first-world society wields as viable currency. Einstein famously described time in the dimensional form, manifesting in a curved relationship with space. Similarly, many Native-American tribes experienced it as circular.[132] I'm not even saying "yes" to this perspective—at least, not in the broad, existential frame. I am choosing to view time as an ally, a friend. In other words, it's personal.

Ultimately, whether we think of time as an abstraction, construct, or tool, it is personal to each of us. We are in a relationship with time. The character of that relationship is most worthy of deliberate exploration. For much of my adult life, I have perceived time as an adversary, a competitor, or, at least, an impediment. And yet, time was never the threat. Mine was unhealthy fear. Unhealthy fear of lost opportunity and relationships. Unhealthy fear of painful rejection. Unhealthy fear of unfulfilled dreams. Under the guise of a type B, take-life-as-it-comes persona, my inner White Rabbit—"I'm late, I'm late! For a very important date!"—waged regular combat.[133] The product of this unholy wrestling has usually been a nice spike of anxiety for me. While the landscape changes when we cross onto untrodden fields in our lives, we often carry old patterns of perceiving with us. I'd like to change that within myself. I'd like to try walking alongside time rather than trying to outrun it, or seeking to lasso and tether it to a fixed place and experience. Maybe, together, time and I will find a few more arrowheads, jutting almost imperceptibly up from newly turned soil.

From a neurological point of view, we experience time primarily in the dorsolateral prefrontal right cortex. Basically, in our foreheads. Our prefrontal cortices are where much of our executive functions reside. This includes our capacity to be present, *truly* present, to our real-time experience. Fortunately, our memories are stored in the hippocampus, buried deep in the lower mid-region of the brain. I like to think this allows us access, via cerebral cross currents, to the fullest relationship with time. In a manner of speaking, time, and time outside of time, offers me the gift of being present, once again, to the here and now and to the simple joys of my childhood. At this moment, it gifts me the chance to say "goodbye" to my daughters while also saying "hello" once again to my old friend Paul. True friends are loyal and attentive. They honor one another. They don't insist on their own way, and they are authentic—authentic and open to finding rhythm and presence with one another. May it be so for me and my traveling companion, Time.

★★★

Oak Ridge was aptly named. In the rolling Piedmont hills of North Carolina, there was a hearty mixture of native pines and other evergreens, along with majestic hardwoods, including numerous oaks. Our backyard was home to two massive scarlet oaks that stood sentinel, reaching over the roof of our simple ranch home as watchful parents, sheltering their brood from threats seen and unseen. As a young boy, I was naturally drawn to these oaks and their coarse beauty, regularly climbing on and about them. The first waiting arms of the trees were about eight feet from the ground. To help me scale the roughly three-to-four-foot-in-diameter trunks, I nailed on a few ascending short sections of one-by-fours to serve as ladder rungs.

Our house had electric baseboard heat but was drafty and poorly insulated. We eventually added a black, cast-iron woodstove in our quaint living room. From then on, this was the warmest room in the house and a place of refuge on cold winter evenings. To keep apace with the requisite supply of cured wood, I spent a few fall and winter Saturdays rummaging fallen-tree sections from the woods. I would then swing a splitting maul in time with my music to cleave the wood into quarters. I tended to stay away from the sappy pines in favor of the cleaner and long-burning oak, hickory, and walnut. The last chore was the stacking of that year's offerings to keep us warm the following winter.

I remember marveling at the inner undulating circles that always told the story of the tree's life. Never perfect, these alternating light and dark concentric rings would invariably include swoops and dips and would have an inner core that was newer, darker, and wetter, leaning and reverberating in one direction, countering the overlay of straighter, outer rings that comprised the earlier years of the tree.

When I reflect on my own life and consider where I am today, and where I hope to be tomorrow, any deliberation, any inner survey, resembles the autobiography of the tree. The tree rings show every season of lean and plenty; every event of fire, plague, or drought; every period of ample rain and alternating sunlight; and the sustenance from the abundant, fertile horizons of loam amidst the rock and red Carolina clay.

I can see, sometimes with painful clarity, the warbled rings of broken relationships in my past, the times when, through the fire of fear, I chose shelter in the supposed safety of false humility, or in response to loss, the faulty choice of diversion on misguided soil. I also can see the times of joy, the fecund seasons when I was visited by vibrancy, grace, and restitution. When I reflect on these times, it is noteworthy that I was involved in the provision of shade and shelter for others and myself.

Today, I am in a good place. To see the composite, the whole history of me, is to see the light and the dark. It matters that I understand the outer rings of my earlier years, those that were once darker and wetter, are now lighter and drier as the result of time, forgiveness, acceptance, and love.

At this moment, I find I am specifically focused in the work of speaking and bringing beauty in numerous creative forms, traditional and relational, into a world rife with strife and discord. As I do this, I need to remind myself the experiences and connections that are yet before me will still come in wet and, at times, dark … all beauty does. I do expect more challenges today and in the days ahead, times of lean, and, of course joys, times of plenty.

Irrespective of what lies ahead, like the stalwart oaks of my youth, I want to, need to, receive these relationships, these events, with equanimity. And, actually—to stretch the metaphor and make it more accurate—rather than following the model of the majestic oak, the spindly Loblolly pine, or the stately walnut, I need to speak from the voice of the aspen which, though appearing to be a stand of numerous trees, is actually one organism. What I do for myself, I do for others; what I do to others, I do to myself. Therefore, I will continue to strive for beauty in and amidst the dark and wet.

★★★

The other day, I was listening to the audiobook version of *The Book of Joy*, an account of a series of conversations between the Dalai Lama and Bishop Desmond Tutu. I heard the Dalai Lama say, "If I were a Christian, I would prefer to go to hell after I die because I may be able to do some good in hell."[134] Stunning. Just stunning words that have quickly imprinted in my mind and heart. While there is so much to unpack within these words, so many angles from which to have long theological and philosophical discussions, I, for now, have settled with considering the very direct and contemporary implications of this idea of doing good in and amongst evil in our world today.

To live is to choose. There are occurrences visited upon us through no choice of ours. This is true. Many of our choices are in response to these events. Growth, at every age, necessarily includes our participation. It's important at different times to delay choice, to rest. But, inevitably, we are called back into the fray, fire, dance, or celebration. Our choice starts with assenting or declining, or asking for a reset, a new hand of cards. Whether we get dealt a new hand, eventually, we have to say "yes" or "no."

When I consider what I have discovered lately about my *yeses* and *nos* in life, my mind goes immediately to the deeply fractured society and world in which we live. The negativity and brokenness are pervasive. Some negativity is part of the natural order, enzymatic to growth and evolution. Some negativity is the result of a different character of brokenness, only attributable to the malevolent energy that is evil.

How do I respond to negativity and brokenness? How do I discern which is organic and which is evil? If my only and absolute response is to indiscriminately cordon off from the negativity, set boundaries, and choose the safety of benevolent and loving individuals, then what is to become of the others who dwell in darkness? If I choose to wade too deeply into the outer darkness in search of ministering to the lost, I risk my own loss of spiritual health and vitality under the enormity of the mission and repeated exposure to the toxins. And who am I to consider I am an arbiter of what is good and what is evil?

As with most things in life, I think of things in terms of dialectics. My need for sustenance and well-being within the community of magnanimous folks is, without question, essential. Many experts in the field of self-help psychology and social work espouse the identifying and removal of toxic people from our lives. But so, too, is my need to respond to the community of folks who are harboring hate, which, short of abject evil, is just a shortcut repository for extreme anger. And anger always arises in the wake of hurt, trespass, and loss. This anger and hurt do not have to be of evil. I believe they most often are not, although, it may certainly devolve into this. As I am a member of the same human and earthly family as these "others," I readily see the zero sum of each group partitioning off into hard separation and exclusion. The ultimate end of this is we all suffer.

The reality of our lives is we are one giant human Venn diagram, or, from the last essay, the Aspen Collective. We are interconnected. But there are times and seasons wherein I may need to say "no" to the work of tending to this interconnectedness. Maybe, in those times, I can and should see myself as the Oak. Or perhaps see these relationships as Chinese linking rings, the old magician's trick where metal rings are clearly interlocked just before the magician pulls once more, and they are cleanly separated. I need both experiences of linkage and separation.

And so, I continue striving to find the alchemy of the two poles: self-care and responding to the needs of others. The other in my life most often really is a mirror image of me—sometimes a vessel, sometimes a maelstrom of love, fear, and hurt. An ultimate irony of life folding back on itself.

To follow the Dalai Lama's lead, if I were a Buddhist, after my death, I would want to be reincarnated as a turkey vulture in my next life. These oft maligned creatures, graceful as they glide along on thermals, go about their work of cleaning out the toxins of rotting death, ultimately making nature clean and beautiful. They are equipped to do so with special enzymes within their GI tracts and on their outer skin to protect them from the harmful bacteria. And they do so with equanimity, without complaint. And in an interesting twist to their work, these vultures gather in what are called "wakes" when they are cleaning carcasses. They will take turns eating, and not everyone will partake. Sometimes, the work needs to be left to others in the community.[135] Would I be good enough in this life to come back as one of them in the next?

★★★

Advice to my Peers
I would prefer to just listen.
If a story came to mind while listening,
I would trust that it is to be shared,
For your benefit and for mine.

And then, again, I would just listen.
I would choose to listen with an open heart,
And if I heard something hurtful from you,
I would love you enough, my fellow traveler,
To speak out and say, "Please stop."

If you ignored my plea, and continued your destructive path,
I would stay with you despite damage to us both.
I would choose to listen with an open heart.
If I heard something that felt hard but productive to us both,
I would thank you for sharing your gift and encourage you
    along the way.

I would choose to listen with an open heart,
And if I heard something from you, which felt joyful,
I would celebrate and dance with you.
But most of all, I would prefer to just listen.
To tell you that you matter.

★★★

Corinthians 13 Redux

We love because we are love.
Forgetting this, we call fear into being
And live for a time cleaved from our own selves.
False piety.
Pharisaic charity.
The aspiration of divine breath.

Love never augers hate
As it holds contradiction in trembling hands.
Love encompasses care and reckless abandon,
And the space between.
It endures and searches,
Like the young shepherd after the lost lamb,
Or a mother elephant keening the remembrance of her dead
  calf.
It seeks and sees itself in the other
And keeps vigil awaiting that recognition.
Love is yoked with truth and therefore isn't always gentle.
It bends.
It breaks.
It yearns for rebirth.
It opens itself to fear, as it seeks to understand
And to be understood.
It is the birthlight of beauty,
Growing amidst shadow and dirt,
Harvesting itself, steadfast
In the lonely work of threshing chaff.
At dusk, Love rests in the arms of itself
Glad for this moment of peace.

Love seeks no comparison,
Only its indigenous self.

ACKNOWLEDGMENTS

In the epilogue of *Finding Beauty in the Gray*, I offer an essay which speaks to the distinctly Western mindset seeking to quantify and bestow the honored titles of "expert" and "brilliance" to persons who create works of art and keen insight in relatively short order. While you, the reader, can decide this particular volume's merits and artistic aplomb, I push back on this Western time filter and impulse. Writing this book has taken the whole of my life to date. Upon even further reflection, I may want to go back to my wonderful editors at Warren Publishing and ask that we edit this particular epilogue essay, changing the single word "me." To be most authentic, the word needs to be "us." It has taken us the whole of my life—and each intersecting person's life—to illuminate and breathe three-dimensional spirit into this book.

This is not to deflect the steady drumbeat of time, focus, energy, and passion I had put forth. I celebrate and take great pride in this book, just as I celebrate and offer my heartfelt gratitude to all those who have contributed right alongside me. Whether actively and directly, or via a more secondary and vicarious process, I have learned an inestimable sum from those who shared their stories with me and continue to do so. Legacy is alive and well, and to the best of my ability, I will carry it forward as a committed link in the ongoing chain of humanity.

I want to begin with offering my love and gratitude to my partner, Heather Lyons. In addition to her overall encouragement and support—no question, she is my biggest cheerleader—she has lent her keen editor's eye to each draft of *Finding Beauty in the Gray*. On the professional side of the ledger, I have appreciated the good folks at Warren Publishing, most especially my developmental editor, Melissa Long. It is clear she and the whole ensemble at Warren see their work through a lens of compassion and integrity within the commitment to high-quality work. They have made the entire process smooth and enjoyable. No slog. Only silk. I am also grateful to my beta readers: Sharon Silcox, Amy Yost, Tina Certo, and Barbara Painter. Your hands have raised this book higher into the light made brighter by your hearts. Various Osher Lifelong Learning Institutes were in on the ground floor of this enterprise, partnering with me and providing me a platform to lead workshops engaging the themes of *Finding Beauty in the Gray*. These good folks, including Kimberly Little and Tina Certo at North Carolina State University and Peter Balsamo at the University of Georgia-Athens, have an unwavering dedication to the lives and spirits of individuals in the second half of life. Finally, I am thankful to my sister, Pam. She is the keeper of our family's stories. She helps distill and clarify my, at times, fuzzy family annals.

The elders of our communities have a great deal more value and treasures of time, heart, and wisdom to offer than many of us (elders themselves included) often consider. It is my hope that, together, we can all reinvigorate our relationships and understandings that everyone, from first breath to last, is vital to the cause of making our world a more beautiful home.

ENDNOTES

1 Steven Spielberg, dir., *Saving Private Ryan* (Hollywood: Paramount Pictures, 1998), 170 min.

2 Jay Kernis, "Lady Bird Johnson, First Lady and Diarist," Sunday Morning, CBS News, March 14, 2021, https://www.cbsnews.com/news/lady-bird-johnson-first-lady-and-diarist/.

3 ———.

4 Rita Mae Brown, *Starting From Scratch: A Different Kind of Writers' Manual* (New York: Bantam Books, 1989), 73.

5 Kernis, "Lady Bird."

6 *Merriam-Webster*, s.v. "retire," https://www.merriam-webster.com/dictionary/retire.

7 Mihaly Csikszentmihalyi, *Flow: The Psychology of Optimal Experience* (New York: Harper Perennial, 1990).

8 "How to Grow Texas Bluebonnets," How-Tos, Lady Bird Johnson Wildflower Center, https://www.wildflower.org/learn/how-to/grow-bluebonnets.

9 Francis Ford Coppola, dir., *Apocalypse Now* (San Francisco: Omni Zoetrope, 1979), 153 min.

10 Viktor E. Frankl, *Man's Search for Meaning* (Boston: Beacon Press, 2006).

11 MetLife Mature Market Institute, *The MetLife Retirement Readiness Index: Are Americans Prepared for the Transition?*, May 2010, https://onlineinvesting.usbank.com/PDF/MMI_Retirement_Readiness_Index_Study.pdf.

12 Boyd Huppert, "WWII Vet Spends COVID-19 Time Weaving 400 Hats for Salvation Army," Land of 10,000 Stories, Kare 11, updated March 15, 2021, https://www.kare11.com/article/news/local/land-of-10000-stories/wwii-vet-spends-covid-time-weaving-hats-for-salvation-army/89-0c07c85f-40b2-4649-b82d-f1572a462456.

13 Shel Silverstein, *The Giving Tree* (New York: HarperCollins, 1999).

14 James Mooney, "Myths of the Cherokees," *Journal of American Folklore* 1, no. 2 (July–September 1888), 97–108, https://doi.org/10.2307/533812.

15 Native Knowledge 360°, "The Trail of Tears: A Story of Cherokee Removal," (online lesson, National Museum of the American Indian, Washington, DC), https://americanindian.si.edu/nk360/resources/The-Trail-of-Tears-A-Story-of-Cherokee-Removal

16 Alex Haley, *Roots: The Saga of an American Family* (New York: Doubleday, 1976).

17 John Heywood, *The Proverbs of John Heywood* (London: Andesite Press, 1874).

18 T. S. Eliot, *Four Quartets* (New York: Harcourt, Brace and Co., 1943).

19 Les Brown, "Shoot for the moon. Even if you miss it, you will land among the stars," Quotable Quotes, Goodreads, https://www.goodreads.com/quotes/1091121-shoot-for-the-moon-even-if-you-miss-you-ll-land.

20 Ray Bradbury, *Fahrenheit 451* (New York: Simon and Schuster, 2012).

21 *Merriam-Webster*, s.v. "legacy," https://www.merriam-webster.com/dictionary/legacy.

22 Elizabeth Arias, PhD et al., *Provisional Life Expectancy Estimates for 2021*, National Vital Statistics System Rapid Release Report 23, August 2022, https://www.cdc.gov/nchs/data/vsrr/vsrr023.pdf.

23 Bruce McIntyre, "A Prayer for the Caregiver," BruceMcIntyre.com, Nov 8, 2013, https://brucemcintyre.com/2013/11/08/a-prayer-for-the-caregiver/.

24 *Oxford English Dictionary*, 2nd ed. (Oxford: Clarendon Press, 1989), s.v. "ambition."

25 *Wikipedia, The Free Encyclopedia*, "Humility," https://en.wikipedia.org/w/index.php?title=Humility&oldid=1134519654.

26 *Oxford English Dictionary*, 2nd ed. (Oxford: Clarendon Press, 1989), s.v. "humility."

27 *Merriam-Webster*, s.v. "humility (n.)," https://www.merriam-webster.com/dictionary/humility.

28 *Wikipedia*, "Humility."

29 Jonathan Star and Shahram Shiva, *A Garden Beyond Paradise: Love Poems of Rumi* (Theone Press, 2006).

30 Daniel Kish, "How I Use Sonar to Navigate the World," filmed March 2015 in New York, NY, TED video, 12:54, https://www.ted.com/talks/daniel_kish_how_i_use_sonar_to_navigate_the_world; and Emerson Foulke, "The Perceptual Basis for Mobility," *American Foundation for the Blind, Research Bulletin* 23 (1971): 1–8.

31 *Merriam-Webster*, s.v. "echolocation," https://www.merriam-webster.com/dictionary/echolocation.

32 "I Yam What I Yam," *Popeye the Sailor*, directed by Dave Fleischer (New York City: Fleischer Studios, 1933), theatrical cartoon short, 6:04 min.

33 MetLife, *Retirement Readiness*.

34 Gene D. Cohen, MD, PhD, *The Creative Age: Awakening Human Potential in the Second Half of Life* (New York City: Quill, 2001).

35 Bruce H. Lipton, PhD, *The Biology of Belief: Unleashing the Power of Consciousness, Matter and Miracles*, rev. ed. (2005; repr., Carlsbad: Hay House, 2015).

36 James A. Horscroft et al., "Metabolic Basis to Sherpa Altitude Adaption," *Proceedings of the National Academy of Sciences* (PNAS) 114, no. 24 (May 2017): 6382–7, https://doi.org/10.1073/pnas.1700527114.

37 Jenny M. Groarke et al., "Loneliness in the UK During the COVID-19 Pandemic: Cross-sectional Results from the COVID-19 Psychological Wellbeing Study," *PLoS ONE* 15, no. 9 (September 2020): e0239698, https://doi.org/10.1371/journal.pone.0239698.

38 Bei Wu, "Social Isolation and Loneliness Among Older Adults in the Context of COVID-19: A Global Challenge," *Global Health Research and Policy* 5, no. 27 (June 2020), https://doi.org/10.1186/s41256-020-00154-3.

39 Brent Bohan, "Intro to Gray Divorce," Gray Divorce (blog), McKinley Irvin Family Law, https://www.mckinleyirvin.com/resources/gray-divorce/.

40 James Wright, *Above the River: The Complete Poems and Selected Prose* (New York: Farrar, Straus and Giroux, 1990), 143.

41 Abraham H. Maslow, "A Theory of Human Motivation," *Psychological Review* 50, no. 4 (1943): 370–96.

42 Ashley E. Smith and Madhu Badireddy, *Failure to Thrive* (Treasure Island, FL: Statpearls Publishing, 2022).

43 Florence Williams, *Heartbreak: A Personal and Scientific Journey* (New York: W. W. Norton & Company, 2022).

44 Wu, "Isolation and Loneliness."

45 Renee Stepler, "Led by Baby Boomers, Divorce Rates Climb for America's 50+ Population," Divorce, Pew Research Center, March 9, 2017, https://www.pewresearch.org/fact-tank/2017/03/09/led-by-baby-boomers-divorce-rates-climb-for-americas-50-population/.

46 Sarah L. Delany, A. Elizabeth Delany, and Amy Hearth, *Having Our Say: The Delany Sisters' First 100 Years* (1993; New York City: Dell Publishing, 1994).

47 ———.

48 *Merriam-Webster*, s.v. "salad days," https://www.merriam-webster.com/dictionary/salad%20days.

49 Tuck Kamin, *Design Your Age: What's Best About You Never Ages* (self-pub., 2015).

50 Suzanne Simard, *Finding the Mother Tree: Discovering the Wisdom of the Forest* (New York: Alfred A. Knopf, 2021).

51 David Lynch, dir., *The Straight Story* (Burbank, CA: Buena Vista Pictures Distribution, 1999).

52 ———.

53 Melvin McLeod, "What Are the Four Noble Truths?" *Lion's Roar*, March 12, 2018, https://www.lionsroar.com/what-are-the-four-noble-truths/.

54 Bill Wilson, *Alcoholics Anonymous: The Big Book* (1939; Mineola, NY: Ixia Press, 2019).

55 Beth McCarthy-Miller, dir., *The Kominsky Method*, season 1, episode 5, "Chapter 5: An Agent Crowns," aired November 16, 2018, on Netflix, https://www.netflix.com/title/80201680.

56 David M. Lee et al., "Sexual Health and Positive Subjective Well-being in Partnered Older Men and Women," *Journals of Gerontology: Series B* 71, no. 4 (July 2016): 698–710, https://doi.org/10.1093/geronb/gbw018.

57 McCarthy-Miller, "An Agent Crowns."

58 Dalia Lama, Desmond Tutu, and Douglas Abrams, *The Book of Joy: Lasting Happiness in a Changing World* (New York: Random, 2016), 122.

59 Haruki Murakami, *What I Talk About When I Talk About Running: A Memoir* (New York: Vintage Books, 2009); and McLeod, "Four Noble Truths."

60 Michelle R. Berman, MD, and Mark S. Boguski, MD, PhD, "Linda Ronstadt's Rare Brain Disorder," Celebrity Diagnosis, *Medpage Today*, January 30, 2020, https://www.medpagetoday.com/popmedicine/celebritydiagnosis/84608.

61 Scott Simon, "Opinion: The Comfort of Cow Cuddles," March 31, 2021, in *Simon Says*, produced by *Weekend Edition Saturday*, NPR podcast, MP3 audio, 2:38, https://www.npr.org/2021/03/13/976631541/opinion-the-comfort-of-cow-cuddles.

62 J. M. Kilner and R. N. Lemon, "What We Know Currently about Mirror Neurons," *Current Biology* 23, no. 23 (December 2013): R1057–62, https://doi.org/10.1016/j.cub.2013.10.051.

63 Greg Miller, "Mirror Neurons May Help Songbirds Stay In Tune," Science 319, no. 5861 (January 2008): 269, https://doi.org/10.1126/science.319.5861.269a.

64 Joan Didion, *The Year of Magical Thinking* (New York: Knopf Doubleday, 2007): 192.

65 ———.

66 Laura Stassi, "Love After Loss," March 25, 2021, in *Dating While Gray*, podcast, MP3 audio, 30:50.

67 ———.

68 Didion, *Magical Thinking*, 55.

69 Elisabeth Kübler-Ross, MD, *On Death and Dying: What the Dying Have to Teach Doctors, Nurses, Clergy, and Their Own Families*, rev. ed. (1976; repr., New York: Scribner, 2014).

70 "Androcles and the Lion," read by Natasha *Storynory*, 6:5, https://smalltalk.fm/ep/KidLit-RADIO-Storynory-ANDROCLES-AND-THE-LION.

71 Jack Donohue, dir., *The Odd Couple*, season 2, episode 17, "You Saved My Life," aired January 21, 1972, on ABC.

72 William Jungenden, dir., *M*A*S*H*, season 6, episode 15, "The Merchant of Korea," aired December 20, 1977, on CBS, https://www.hulu.com/mash.

73 "Giving Thanks Can Make You Happier," Harvard Medical School, Harvard Health Publishing, August 14, 2021, https://www.health.harvard.edu/healthbeat/giving-thanks-can-make-you-happier.

74 A. J. Jacobs, *Thanks a Thousand: A Gratitude Journey* (New York: TED Books, Simon & Schuster, 2018).

75 ———, "The Gratitude Chain," February 19, 2021, in *TED Radio Hour*, produced by NPR, podcast, 51:33, https://www.npr.org/2021/02/18/969032187/the-gratitude-chain-a-j-jacobs.

76 ———.

77 ———.

78 The Princeton Language Institute, ed., *Roget's 21st Century Thesaurus in Dictionary Form*, 3rd ed. (New York: Dell Publishing Company, Inc., 2005).

79 "David Driskell: Icons of Nature and History," Art & Exhibitions, Portland Museum of Art, https://www.portlandmuseum.org/driskell.

80 Jackie Rocheleau, "15 Basic Physics Concepts to Help You Understand Our World," Space, Stacker, October 6, 2021, https://stacker.com/space/15-basic-physics-concepts-help-you-understand-our-world.

81 *Wikipedia, The Free Encyclopedia*, "Inertia," https://en.wikipedia.org/w/index.php?title=Inertia&oldid=1137528743.

82 ———, "Entropy," https://en.wikipedia.org/w/index.php?title=Entropy&oldid=1140458240.

83 ———, "Meson," https://en.wikipedia.org/w/index.php?title=Meson&oldid=1141018062.

84 Lipton, *Biology of Belief*.

85 Chris Matthews, *Tip and the Gipper: When Politics Worked* (New York: Simon & Schuster Paperbacks, 2013), 61, 129.

86 Norman Doidge, MD, *The Brain That Changes Itself: Stories of Personal Triumph from the Frontiers of Brain Science* (New York: Penguin Books, 2007).

87 ———.

88 Manoush Zomordi, Diba Mohtasham, and Sanaz Meshkinpour, "Julia Watson: What Can We Learn From Indigenous Design Developed Over Generations?" February 5, 2021, in It Takes Time, produced by *TED Radio Hour*, NPR podcast, MP3 audio, 11:22, https://www.npr.org/2021/02/05/964214673/julia-watson-what-can-we-learn-from-indigineous-design-developed-over-generation.

89   "What Is Workamping?" About Workamping *Workamper News*, https://www.workamper.com/workamper-article/what-workamping#:~:text=Workampers%20are%20adventuresome%20individuals%2C%20couples,time%20work%20with%20RV%20camping.

90   Chloé Zhao, dir., *Nomadland* (Los Angelas: Searchlight Pictures, 2020), https://www.hulu.com/movie/nomadland.

91   ———.

92   ———.

93   Jessica Bruder, interview by Jeffrey Brown, *Brown/Vinopal NewsHour*, PBS, April 15, 2021.

94   "Participating in the Arts Creates Paths to Healthy Aging," National Institute on Aging, February 15, 2019, https://www.nia.nih.gov/news/participating-arts-creates-paths-healthy-aging.

95   Andrew Stanton, dir., *Finding Nemo* (Burbank, CA: Buena Vista Pictures, 2003), https://www.disneyplus.com/movies/finding-nemo.

96   *Wikipedia, The Free Encyclopedia*, "Elizabeth Cotten," https://en.wikipedia.org/w/index.php?title=Elizabeth_Cotten&oldid=1137859103.

97   Barry Schwartz, *The Paradox of Choice: Why More is Less* (New York City, Ecco Press, 2004).

98   *Wikipedia, The Free Encyclopedia*, "Curiosity (rover)," https://en.wikipedia.org/w/index.php?title=Curiosity_(rover)&oldid=1138595819.

99   Clara Ma, excerpt from "Curiosity," *Nasa Science: Mars Exploration*, NASA, May, 27, 2009, https://mars.nasa.gov/namerover/WinnerAnnouncedEssay/.

100 "Youth Is Wasted on the Young," Tracing Quotations, Quote Investigators, September 7, 2015, https://quoteinvestigator.com/2015/09/07/young/.

101 Road Scholar, created by Elderhostel, is a nonprofit leader in lifelong experiential-learning opportunities worldwide. To learn more, visit www.roadscholar.org.

102 *Merriam-Webster*, s.v. "archetype," https://www.merriam-webster.com/dictionary/archetype.

103 Mel Stuart, dir., *Willy Wonka & the Chocolate Factory* (Hollywood: Paramount, 1971), videocassette (VHS), 100 min.

104 Leslie Bricusse and Anthony Newley, "Pure Imagination," in *Roald Dahl's Willy Wonka* by Tim McDonald and Leslie Bricusse (New York: Music Theatre International, 2004).

105 "The Day That the Stars Bent for Einstein," *The Saturday Evening Post*, March 20, 2010, https://www.saturdayeveningpost.com/sep-keyword/albert-einstein/.

106 Ronald Devere, MD, "Music and Dementia: An Overview," *Practical Neurology*, June 2017, https://practicalneurology.com/articles/2017-june/music-and-dementia-an-overview.

107 Sandrine Vieillard and Anne-Laure Gilet, "Age-related Differences in Affective Responses to and Memory for Emotions Conveyed by Music: A Cross-sectional Study," *Frontiers in Psychology* 4 (October 2013): 711, https://doi.org/10.3389/fpsyg.2013.00711.

108 Samuel A. Mehr et al., "Universality and Diversity in Human Song," *Science* 366, no. 6468 (November 2019), https://doi.org/10.1126/science.aax0868.

109 Rebecca Gilbert, "Music Therapy and Other Complimentary Therapies For Parkinson's," Parkinson's Treatments, American Parkinson Disease Association, February 5, 2019, https://www.apdaparkinson.org/article/music-therapy-parkinsons-disease/.

110 Tom Shadyac, dir., *Patch Adams* (Universal City: Universal Pictures, 1998), videocassette (VHS), 115 min.

111 ———.

112 Mary Oliver, *Upstream: Selected Essays* (New York: Penguin Press, 2016).

113 Ryan W. Miller, "Baarack, a Sheep Rescued in Australia With Over 75 Pounds of Wool, Is 'Getting More Confident Every Day,'" *USA Today*, February 25, 2021.

114 Shadyac, *Patch Adams*.

115 Jayne Leonard, "What Is Learned Helplessness?" reviewed by Danielle Wade, *Medical News Today*, updated September 2, 2022, https://www.medicalnewstoday.com/articles/325355.

116 Deborah Fulghum Bruce, PhD, "Depression in Older People," reviewed by Jennifer Casarella, MD, Guide, WebMD, September 4, 2022, https://www.webmd.com/depression/guide/depression-elderly; and Wyatt Koma et al., "One in Four Older Adults Report Anxiety or Depression Amid the COVID-19 Pandemic," Henry J. Kaiser Family Foundation, October 9, 2020, https://www.kff.org/medicare/issue-brief/one-in-four-older-adults-report-anxiety-or-depression-amid-the-covid-19-pandemic/.

117 Saul McLeod, PhD, "Attribution Theory—Situational vs Dispositional," reviewed by Olivia Guy-Evans, Social Science, *Simply Psychology*, updated February 8, 2023, www.simplypsychology.org/attribution-theory.html.

118 William J. Chopik, Eric S. Kim, and Jacqui Smith, "Changes in Optimism Are Associated with Changes in Health Over Time Among Older Adults," *Social Psychological and Personality Science* 6, no. 7 (June 2015): 814–22, https://doi.org/10.1177/1948550615590199; and Martin E. P. Seligman, PhD, *Learned Optimism: How to Change Your Mind and Your Life* (New York: Vintage, 2006).

119 Angela Thoreson, "Helping People, Changing Lives: Three Health Benefits of Volunteering," Speaking of Health, Mayo Clinic Health System, September 16, 2021, https://www.mayoclinichealthsystem.org/hometown-health/speaking-of-health/3-health-benefits-of-volunteering.

120 Jill LePore, "Ruth Bader Ginsburg, The Great Equalizer: How a Scholar, Advocate, and Judge Upended the Entirety of American Political Thought," *New Yorker*, September 18, 2020, https://www.newyorker.com/news/postscript/ruth-bader-ginsburg-supreme-court-the-great-equalizer-obituary; and Alexander Kacala, "20 Inspiring and Empowering Quotes from the Late Ruth Bader Ginsburg," *Today*, September 18, 2020, https://www.today.com/news/ruth-bader-ginsburg-quotes-20-inspiring-ideas-rbg-t192057.

121 Reynolds, Gene, dir., *M*A*S*H*, season 1, episode 12, "Dear Dad," aired December 17, 1972, on CBS, https://www.hulu.com/mash.

122 David Carson, dir., *Northern Exposure*, season 2, episode 7, "Slow Dance," aired May 20, 1991, on CBS.

123 Sharon Martin, "How Addiction Impacts the Family: 6 Family Roles in a Dysfunctional or Alcoholic Family," *Psych Central*, May 15, 2017, https://psychcentral.com/blog/imperfect/2017/05/how-addiction-impacts-the-family-6-family-roles-in-a-dysfunctional-or-alcoholic-family.

124 Tom Magliozzi and Ray Magliozzi, "Say It: 'Arup Gupta,'" *Car Talk*, produced by Doug Berman, February 5, 1994, Boston, MA, radio broadcast, Adobe Flash audio, 58:32, https://www.cartalk.com/radio/show/9406-say-it-arup-gupta.

125 Thomas Dambo, "The Great Story of the Little People and the Giant Trolls," Events and Exhibits, Coastal Maine Botanical Gardens, https://www.mainegardens.org/events-exhibits/giant-trolls/.

126 ———.

127 "Meet Our Trolls," Events and Exhibits, Coastal Maine Botanical Gardens, https://www.mainegardens.org/events-exhibits/giant-trolls/meet-our-trolls/.

128 Robert Zemeckis, dir., *Forrest Gump* (Hollywood: Paramount Pictures, 1994), videocassette (VHS), 142 min.

129 Jack Maden, "John Locke's Empiricism: Why We Are All Tabula Rasas (Blank Slates)," *Philosophy Break*, March 2021, https://philosophybreak.com/articles/john-lockes-empiricism-why-we-are-all-tabula-rasas-blank-slates/.

130 Irving Stone and Jean Stone, eds., *Dear Theo: The Autobiography of Vincent Van Gogh* (New York: Plume, 1995).

131 "This One's for You: The Story Behind Elton John's Hit 'Your Song,'" *Independent*, November 15, 2018, https://www.independent.co.uk/arts-entertainment/music/features/elton-john-your-song-john-lewis-christmas-advert-2018-history-bernie-taupin-a8634866.html.

132 Nola Taylor Tillman, Meghan Bartels, and Scott Dutfield, "Einstein's Theory of General Relativity," Science & Astronomy, Space.com, updated January 13, 2022, https://www.space.com/17661-theory-general-relativity.html.

133 Clyde Geronimi, Wilfred Jackson, and Hamilton Luske, *Alice in Wonderland* (Burbank, CA: Walt Disney Productions, 1951), videocassette (VHS), 75 min.

134 Dalai Lama, Desmond Tutu, and Douglas Abrams, *The Book of Joy: Lasting Happiness in a Changing World*, read by Douglas Abrams, Francois Chau, and Peter Francis James (New York: Penguin Audio, 2016), audiobook, 10 hr., 12 min.

135 "NETN Species Spotlight-Turkey and Black Vultures," Article, National Park Service, updated August 15, 2021, https://www.nps.gov/articles/netn-species-spotlight-vultures.htm.

BIBLIOGRAPHY

"Androcles and the Lion." Read by Natasha *Storynory*, 6:5. https://smalltalk.fm/ep/KidLit-RADIO-Storynory-ANDROCLES-AND-THE-LION.

"David Driskell: Icons of Nature and History." Art & Exhibitions. Portland Museum of Art. https://www.portlandmuseum.org/driskell.

"Giving Thanks Can Make You Happier." Harvard Medical School. Harvard Health Publishing. August 14, 2021. https://www.health.harvard.edu/healthbeat/giving-thanks-can-make-you-happier.

"How to Grow Texas Bluebonnets." How-Tos. Lady Bird Johnson Wildflower Center. https://www.wildflower.org/learn/how-to/grow-bluebonnets.

"I Yam What I Yam." *Popeye the Sailor*. Directed by Dave Fleischer. New York City: Fleischer Studios, 1933. Theatrical cartoon short, 6:04 min.

"Meet Our Trolls." Events and Exhibits. Coastal Maine Botanical Gardens. https://www.mainegardens.org/events-exhibits/giant-trolls/meet-our-trolls/.

"NETN Species Spotlight-Turkey and Black Vultures." Article. National Park Service. Updated August 15, 2021. https://www.nps.gov/articles/netn-species-spotlight-vultures.htm.

"Participating in the Arts Creates Paths to Healthy Aging." National Institute on Aging. February 15, 2019. https://www.nia.nih.gov/news/participating-arts-creates-paths-healthy-aging.

"The Day That the Stars Bent for Einstein." *The Saturday Evening Post*. March 20, 2010. https://www.saturdayeveningpost.com/sep-keyword/albert-einstein/.

"This One's for You: The Story Behind Elton John's Hit 'Your Song.'" *Independent*. November 15, 2018. https://www.independent.co.uk/arts-entertainment/music/features/elton-john-your-song-john-lewis-christmas-advert-2018-history-bernie-taupin-a8634866.html.

"What Is Workamping?" About Workamping *Workamper News*. https://www.workamper.com/workamper-article/what-workamping#:~:text=Workampers%20are%20adventuresome%20individuals%2C%20couples,time%20work%20with%20RV%20camping.

"Youth Is Wasted on the Young." Tracing Quotations. Quote Investigators. September 7, 2015. https://quoteinvestigator.com/2015/09/07/young/.

Arias, Elizabeth, PhD, Betzaida Tejada-Vera, MS, Kenneth D. Kochanek, MA, and Farida B. Ahmad, MPH. *Provisional Life Expectancy Estimates for 2021*. National Vital Statistics System Rapid Release Report 23. August 2022. https://www.cdc.gov/nchs/data/vsrr/vsrr023.pdf.

Berman, Michelle R., MD, and Mark S. Boguski, MD, PhD. "Linda Ronstadt's Rare Brain Disorder." Celebrity Diagnosis. *Medpage Today*. January 30, 2020. https://www.medpagetoday.com/popmedicine/celebritydiagnosis/84608.

Bohan, Brent. "Intro to Gray Divorce." Gray Divorce (blog). McKinley Irvin Family Law. https://www.mckinleyirvin.com/resources/gray-divorce/.

Bradbury, Ray. *Fahrenheit 451*. New York: Simon and Schuster, 2012.

Bricusse, Leslie, and Anthony Newley. "Pure Imagination," in *Roald Dahl's Willy Wonka* by Tim McDonald and Leslie Bricusse. New York: Music Theatre International, 2004.

Brown, Les. "Shoot for the moon. Even if you miss it, you will land among the stars." Quotable Quotes. Goodreads. https://www.goodreads.com/quotes/1091121-shoot-for-the-moon-even-if-you-miss-you-ll-land.

Brown, Rita Mae. *Starting From Scratch: A Different Kind of Writers' Manual*. New York: Bantam Books, 1989. 73.

Bruce, Deborah Fulghum, PhD. "Depression in Older People." Reviewed by Jennifer Casarella, MD. Guide. WebMD. September 4, 2022. https://www.webmd.com/depression/guide/depression-elderly.

Bruder, Jessica. Interview by Jeffrey Brown. *Brown/Vinopal NewsHour*. PBS. April 15, 2021.

Carson, David, dir. *Northern Exposure*. Season 2, episode 7, "Slow Dance." Aired May 20, 1991, on CBS.

Chopik, William J., Eric S. Kim, and Jacqui Smith. "Changes in Optimism Are Associated with Changes in Health Over Time Among Older Adults." *Social Psychological and Personality Science* 6, no. 7 (June 2015): 814–22, https://doi.org/10.1177/1948550615590199.

Cohen, Gene D., MD, PhD. *The Creative Age: Awakening Human Potential in the Second Half of Life*. New York City: Quill, 2001.

Coppola, Francis Ford, dir. *Apocalypse Now*. San Francisco: Omni Zoetrope, 1979. 153 min.

Csikszentmihalyi, Mihaly. *Flow: The Psychology of Optimal Experience*. New York: Harper Perennial, 1990.

Dambo, Thomas. "The Great Story of the Little People and the Giant Trolls." Events and Exhibits. Coastal Maine Botanical Gardens. https://www.mainegardens.org/events-exhibits/giant-trolls/.

Delany, Sarah L., A. Elizabeth Delany, and Amy Hearth. *Having Our Say: The Delany Sisters' First 100 Years*. New York City: Dell Publishing, 1994. First published 1993.

Devere, Ronald, MD. "Music and Dementia: An Overview." *Practical Neurology*. June 2017. https://practicalneurology.com/articles/2017-june/music-and-dementia-an-overview.

Didion, Joan. *The Year of Magical Thinking*. New York: Knopf Doubleday, 2007. 55.

———, 192.

Doidge, Norman, MD. *The Brain That Changes Itself: Stories of Personal Triumph from the Frontiers of Brain Science*. New York: Penguin Books, 2007.

Donohue, Jack, dir. *The Odd Couple*. Season 2, episode 17, "You Saved My Life." Aired January 21, 1972, on ABC.

Eliot, T. S. *Four Quartets*. New York: Harcourt, Brace and Co., 1943.

Foulke, Emerson. "The Perceptual Basis for Mobility." *American Foundation for the Blind, Research Bulletin* 23 (1971): 1–8.

Frankl, Viktor E. *Man's Search for Meaning*. Boston: Beacon Press, 2006.

Geronimi, Clyde, Wilfred Jackson, and Hamilton Luske. *Alice in Wonderland*. Burbank, CA: Walt Disney Productions, 1951. Videocassette (VHS), 75 min.

Gilbert, Rebecca. "Music Therapy and Other Complimentary Therapies For Parkinson's." Parkinson's Treatments. American Parkinson Disease Association. February 5, 2019. https://www.apdaparkinson.org/article/music-therapy-parkinsons-disease/.

Groarke, Jenny M., Emma Berry, Lisa Graham-Wisener, Phoebe E. McKenna-Plumley, Emily McGlinchey, and Cherie Armour. "Loneliness in the UK During the COVID-19 Pandemic: Cross-sectional Results from the COVID-19 Psychological Wellbeing Study." *PLoS ONE* 15, no. 9 (September 2020): e0239698. https://doi.org/10.1371/journal.pone.0239698.

Haley, Alex. Roots: *The Saga of an American Family*. New York: Doubleday, 1976.

Heywood, John. *The Proverbs of John Heywood: Being the "Proverbes" of that Author, Printed 1546*. London: Andesite Press, 1874.

Horscroft, James A., Aleksandra O. Kotwica, Verena Laner, James A. West, Philip J. Hennis, Denny Z. H. Levett, David J. Howard, Bernadette O. Fernandez, Sarah L. Burgess, Zsuzsanna Ament, Edward T. Gilbert-Kawai, André Vercueil, Blaine D. Landis, Kay Mitchell, Monty G. Mythen, Cristina Branco, Randall S. Johnson, Martin Feelisch, Hugh E. Montgomery, Julian L. Griffin, Michael P. W. Grocott, Erich Gnaiger, Daniel S. Martin, and Andrew J. Murray. "Metabolic Basis to Sherpa Altitude Adaption." *Proceedings of the National Academy of Sciences* (PNAS) 114, no. 24 (May 2017): 6382–7. https://doi.org/10.1073/pnas.1700527114.

Huppert, Boyd. "WWII Vet Spends COVID-19 Time Weaving 400 Hats for Salvation Army." Land of 10,000 Stories. Kare 11. Updated March 15, 2021. https://www.kare11.com/article/news/local/land-of-10000-stories/wwii-vet-spends-covid-time-weaving-hats-for-salvation-army/89-0c07c85f-40b2-4649-b82d-f1572a462456.

Jacobs, A. J. "The Gratitude Chain." February 19, 2021, in *TED Radio Hour*. Produced by NPR. Podcast, 51:33. https://www.npr.org/2021/02/18/969032187/the-gratitude-chain-a-j-jacobs.

Jacobs, A. J. *Thanks a Thousand: A Gratitude Journey*. New York: TED Books, Simon & Schuster, 2018.

Jungenden, William, dir. *M*A*S*H*. Season 6, episode 15, "The Merchant of Korea." Aired December 20, 1977, on CBS, https://www.hulu.com/mash.

Kacala, Alexander. "20 Inspiring and Empowering Quotes from the Late Ruth Bader Ginsburg." *Today*. September 18, 2020. https://www.today.com/news/ruth-bader-ginsburg-quotes-20-inspiring-ideas-rbg-t192057.

Kamin, Tuck. *Design Your Age: What's Best About You Never Ages.* Self-pub., 2015.

Kernis, Jay. "Lady Bird Johnson, First Lady and Diarist." Sunday Morning. CBS News. March 14, 2021. https://www.cbsnews.com/news/lady-bird-johnson-first-lady-and-diarist/.

Kilner, J. M., and R. N. Lemon. "What We Know Currently about Mirror Neurons." *Current Biology* 23, no. 23 (December 2013): R1057–62. https://doi.org/10.1016/j.cub.2013.10.051.

Kish, Daniel. "How I Use Sonar to Navigate the World." Filmed March 2015 in New York, NY. TED video, 12:54. https://www.ted.com/talks/daniel_kish_how_i_use_sonar_to_ navigate_the_world.

Koma, Wyatt, Sarah True, Jeannie Fuglesten Biniek, Juliette Cubanski, Kendal Orgera, and Rachel Garfield. "One in Four Older Adults Report Anxiety or Depression Amid the COVID-19 Pandemic." Henry J. Kaiser Family Foundation. October 9, 2020. https://www.kff.org/medicare/issue-brief/one-in-four-older-adults-report-anxiety-or-depression-amid-the-covid-19-pandemic/.

Kübler-Ross, Elisabeth, MD. *On Death and Dying: What the Dying Have to Teach Doctors, Nurses, Clergy, and Their Own Families.* London: Macmillan, 1976. Reprinted with an introduction by Ira Byock, MD. New York: Scribner, 2014. Page references are to the 2014 edition.

Lama, Dalai, Desmond Tutu, and Douglas Abrams. *The Book of Joy: Lasting Happiness in a Changing World.* New York: Random, 2016. 122.

———. Read by Douglas Abrams, Francois Chau, and Peter Francis James. New York: Penguin Audio, 2016. Audiobook, 10 hr., 12 min.

Lee, David M., Bram Vanhoutte, James Nazroo, and Neil Pendleton. "Sexual Health and Positive Subjective Well-being in Partnered Older Men and Women." *Journals of Gerontology: Series B* 71, no. 4 (July 2016): 698–710. https://doi.org/10.1093/geronb/gbw018.

Leonard, Jayne. "What Is Learned Helplessness?" Reviewed by Danielle Wade. *Medical News Today.* Updated September 2, 2022. https://www.medicalnewstoday.com/articles/325355.

LePore, Jill. "Ruth Bader Ginsburg, The Great Equalizer: How a Scholar, Advocate, and Judge Upended the Entirety of American Political Thought." *New Yorker.* September 18, 2020. https://www.newyorker.com/news/postscript/ruth-bader-ginsburg-supreme-court-the-great-equalizer-obituary.

Lipton, Bruce H., PhD. *The Biology of Belief: Unleashing the Power of Consciousness, Matter and Miracles.* Self-pub., 2005. Reprinted with an expansion. Carlsbad: Hay House, 2015. Page references are to the 2015 edition.

Lynch, David, dir. *The Straight Story.* Burbank, CA: Buena Vista Pictures Distribution, 1999.

Ma, Clara. Excerpt from "Curiosity." *Nasa Science: Mars Exploration.* NASA. May, 27, 2009. https://mars.nasa.gov/namerover/WinnerAnnouncedEssay/.

Maden, Jack. "John Locke's Empiricism: Why We Are All Tabula Rasas (Blank Slates)." *Philosophy Break.* March 2021. https://philosophybreak.com/articles/john-lockes-empiricism-why-we-are-all-tabula-rasas-blank-slates/.

Magliozzi, Tom, and Ray Magliozzi. "Say It: 'Arup Gupta.'" *Car Talk.* Produced by Doug Berman. February 5, 1994. Boston, MA. Radio broadcast. Adobe Flash audio, 58:32, https://www.cartalk.com/radio/show/9406-say-it-arup-gupta.

Martin, Sharon. "How Addiction Impacts the Family: 6 Family Roles in a Dysfunctional or Alcoholic Family." *Psych Central.* May 15, 2017. https://psychcentral.com/blog/imperfect/2017/05/how-addiction-impacts-the-family-6-family-roles-in-a-dysfunctional-or-alcoholic-family.

Maslow, Abraham H. "A Theory of Human Motivation." *Psychological Review* 50, no. 4 (1943): 370–96.

Matthews, Chris. *Tip and the Gipper: When Politics Worked.* New York: Simon & Schuster Paperbacks, 2013. 61, 129.

McCarthy-Miller, Beth, dir. *The Kominsky Method.* Season 1, episode 5, "Chapter 5: An Agent Crowns." Aired November 16, 2018, on Netflix. https://www.netflix.com/title/80201680.

McIntyre, Bruce. "A Prayer for the Caregiver." *BruceMcIntyre.com. Nov 8, 2013. https://brucemcintyre.com/2013/11/08/a-prayer-for-the-caregiver/.*

McLeod, Melvin. "What Are the Four Noble Truths?" *Lion's Roar.* March 12, 2018. https://www.lionsroar.com/what-are-the-four-noble-truths/.

McLeod, Saul, PhD. "Attribution Theory—Situational vs Dispositional." Reviewed by Olivia Guy-Evans. Social Science. *Simply Psychology.* Updated February 8, 2023. www.simplypsychology.org/attribution-theory.html.

Mehr, Samuel A., Manvir Singh, Dean Knox, Daniel M. Ketter, Daniel Pickens-Jones, S. Atwood, Christopher Lucas, Nori Jacoby, Alena A. Egner, Erin J. Hopkins, Rhea M. Howard, Joshua K. Hartshorne, Mariela V. Jennings, Jan Simson, Constance M. Bainbridge, Steven Pinker, Timothy J. O'Donnell, Max M. Krasnow, and Luke Glowacki. "Universality and Diversity in Human Song." *Science* 366, no. 6468 (November 2019). https://doi.org/10.1126/science.aax0868.

Merriam-Webster, s.v. "Archetype." https://www.merriam-webster.com/dictionary/archetype.

———. "Echolocation." https://www.merriam-webster.com/dictionary/echolocation.

———. "Humility (*n.*)." https://www.merriam-webster.com/dictionary/humility.

———. "Legacy." https://www.merriam-webster.com/dictionary/legacy.

———. "Retire." https://www.merriam-webster.com/dictionary/retire.

———. "Salad days." https://www.merriam-webster.com/dictionary/salad%20days.

MetLife Mature Market Institute. *The MetLife Retirement Readiness Index: Are Americans Prepared for the Transition?* May 2010. https://onlineinvesting.usbank.com/PDF/MMI_Retirement_Readiness_Index_Study.pdf.

Miller, Greg. "Mirror Neurons May Help Songbirds Stay In Tune." *Science* 319, no. 5861 (January 2008): 269. https://doi.org/10.1126/science.319.5861.269a.

Miller, Ryan W. "Baarack, a Sheep Rescued in Australia With Over 75 Pounds of Wool, Is 'Getting More Confident Every Day.'" *USA Today.* February 25, 2021.

Mooney, James. "Myths of the Cherokees." *Journal of American Folklore* 1, no. 2 (July–September 1888), 97–108. https://doi.org/10.2307/533812.

Murakami, Haruki. *What I Talk About When I Talk About Running: A Memoir*. New York: Vintage Books, 2009.

Native Knowledge 360°. "The Trail of Tears: A Story of Cherokee Removal." Online lesson. National Museum of the American Indian. https://americanindian.si.edu/nk360/resources/The-Trail-of-Tears-A-Story-of-Cherokee-Removal.

Oliver, Mary. *Upstream: Selected Essays*. New York: Penguin Press, 2016.

Oxford English Dictionary, 2nd ed. Oxford: Clarendon Press, 1989, s.v. "Ambition."

———. "Humility."

Reynolds, Gene, dir. *M*A*S*H*. Season 1, episode 12, "Dear Dad." Aired December 17, 1972, on CBS. https://www.hulu.com/mash.

Rocheleau, Jackie. "15 Basic Physics Concepts to Help You Understand Our World." Space, Stacker. October 6, 2021. https://stacker.com/space/15-basic-physics-concepts-help-you-understand-our-world.

Schwartz, Barry. *The Paradox of Choice: Why More is Less*. New York City, Ecco Press, 2004.

Seligman, Martin E. P., PhD. *Learned Optimism: How to Change Your Mind and Your Life*. New York: Vintage, 2006.

Shadyac, Tom, dir. *Patch Adams*. Universal City: Universal Pictures, 1998. Videocassette (VHS), 115 min.

Silverstein, Shel. *The Giving Tree*. New York: HarperCollins, 1999.

Simard, Suzanne. *Finding the Mother Tree: Discovering the Wisdom of the Forest*. New York: Alfred A. Knopf, 2021.

Simon, Scott. "Opinion: The Comfort of Cow Cuddles." March 31, 2021, in *Simon Says*. Produced by *Weekend Edition Saturday*. NPR podcast. MP3 audio, 2:38. https://www.npr.org/2021/03/13/976631541/opinion-the-comfort-of-cow-cuddles.

Smith, Ashley E., and Madhu Badireddy. *Failure to Thrive*. Treasure Island, FL: Statpearls Publishing, 2022.

Spielberg, Steven, dir. *Saving Private Ryan*. Hollywood: Paramount Pictures, 1998. 170 min.

Stanton, Andrew, dir. *Finding Nemo*. Burbank, CA: Buena Vista Pictures, 2003. https://www.disneyplus.com/movies/finding-nemo.

Star, Jonathan, and Shahram Shiva. *A Garden Beyond Paradise: Love Poems of Rumi*. Theone Press, 2006.

Stassi, Laura. "Love After Loss," March 25, 2021, in *Dating While Gray*. Podcast. MP3 audio, 30:50.

Stepler, Renee. "Led by Baby Boomers, Divorce Rates Climb for America's 50+ Population." Divorce. Pew Research Center. March 9, 2017. https://www.pewresearch.org/fact-tank/2017/03/09/led-by-baby-boomers-divorce-rates-climb-for-americas-50-population/.

Stone, Irving, and Jean Stone, eds. *Dear Theo: The Autobiography of Vincent Van Gogh*. New York: Plume, 1995.

Stuart, Mel, dir. *Willy Wonka & the Chocolate Factory*. Hollywood: Paramount, 1971. Videocassette (VHS), 100 min.

The Princeton Language Institute, ed.. *Roget's 21st Century Thesaurus in Dictionary Form*, 3rd ed. New York: Dell Publishing Company, Inc., 2005.

Thoreson, Angela. "Helping People, Changing Lives: Three Health Benefits of Volunteering." Speaking of Health. Mayo Clinic Health System. September 16, 2021. https://www.mayoclinichealthsystem.org/hometown-health/speaking-of-health/3-health-benefits-of-volunteering.

Tillman, Nola Taylor, Meghan Bartels, and Scott Dutfield. "Einstein's Theory of General Relativity." Science & Astronomy. Space.com. Updated January 13, 2022. https://www.space.com/17661-theory-general-relativity.html.

Vieillard, Sandrine, and Anne-Laure Gilet. "Age-related Differences in Affective Responses to and Memory for Emotions Conveyed by Music: A Cross-sectional Study." *Frontiers in Psychology* 4 (October 2013): 711. https://doi.org/10.3389/fpsyg.2013.00711.

Wikipedia, The Free Encyclopedia. "Curiosity (rover)." https://en.wikipedia.org/w/index.php?title=Curiosity_(rover)&oldid=1138595819.

———. "Elizabeth Cotten." https://en.wikipedia.org/w/index.php?title=Elizabeth_Cotten&oldid=1137859103.

———. "Entropy." https://en.wikipedia.org/w/index.php?title=Entropy&oldid=1140458240.

———. "Humility." https://en.wikipedia.org/w/index.php?title=Humility&oldid=1134519654.

———. "Inertia." https://en.wikipedia.org/w/index.php?title=Inertia&oldid=1137528743.

———. "Meson." https://en.wikipedia.org/w/index.php?title=Meson&oldid=1141018062.

Williams, Florence. *Heartbreak: A Personal and Scientific Journey*. New York: W. W. Norton & Company, 2022.

Wilson, Bill. *Alcoholics Anonymous: The Big Book*. Mineola, NY: Ixia Press, 2019. First published 1939.

Wright, James. *Above the River: The Complete Poems and Selected Prose*. New York: Farrar, Straus and Giroux, 1990. 143.

Wu, Bei. "Social Isolation and Loneliness Among Older Adults in the Context of COVID-19: A Global Challenge." *Global Health Research and Policy* 5, no. 27 (June 2020). https://doi.org/10.1186/s41256-020-00154-3.

Zemeckis, Robert, dir.. *Forrest Gump*. Hollywood: Paramount Pictures, 1994. Videocassette (VHS), 142 min.

Zhao, Chloé, dir. *Nomadland*. Los Angelas: Searchlight Pictures, 2020. https://www.hulu.com/movie/nomadland.

Zomordi, Manoush, Diba Mohtasham, and Sanaz Meshkinpour. "Julia Watson: What Can We Learn From Indigenous Design Developed Over Generations?" February 5, 2021, in *It Takes Time*. Produced by *TED Radio Hour*. NPR podcast. MP3 audio, 11:22. https://www.npr.org/2021/02/05/964214673/julia-watson-what-can-we-learn-from-indigineous-design-developed-over-generation.